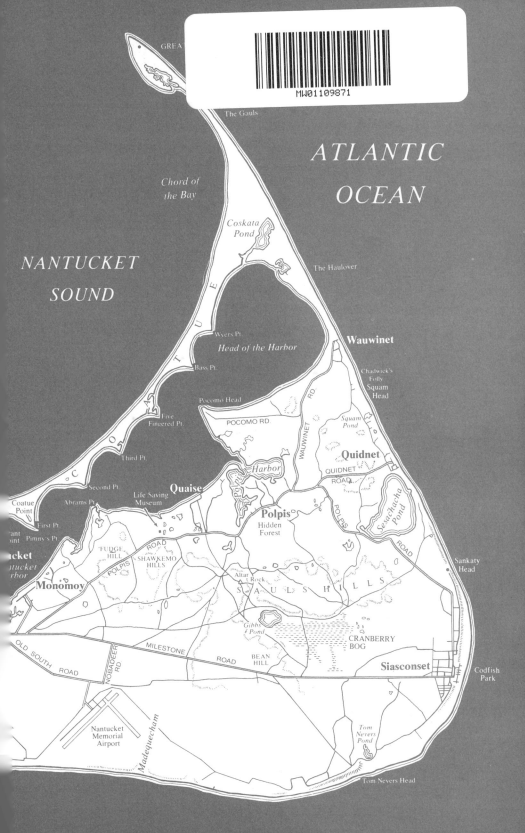

ATLANTIC

OCEAN

NANTUCKET

SOUND

GREAT

The Gauls

MW01109871

Chord of
the Bay

Coskata
Pond

The Haulover

Wyers Pt.

Head of the Harbor

Wauwinet

Bass Pt.

Chadwick's
Folly
Squam
Head

Pocomo Head

POCOMO RD.

Squam
Pond

Five
Fingered Pt.

Quidnet

QUIDNET

Third Pt.

Harbor

ROAD

Second Pt.

Quaise

Life Saving
Museum

Polpis

POLPIS

Sesachacha
Pond

Coatue
Point

Abrams Pt.

Hidden
Forest

ROAD

First Pt.

Pimny's Pt.

'FUDGE'
HILL

POLPIS

SHAWKEMO
HILLS

ROAD

Sankaty
Head

cket

tucket
rbor

Monomoy

Altar
Rock

SAUL S HILLS

Gibbs
Pond

CRANBERRY
BOG

OLD SOUTH ROAD

MILESTONE

NOBADEER RD

BEAN
HILL

ROAD

Siasconset

Codfish
Park

Nantucket
Memorial
Airport

Madequecham

Tom
Nevers
Pond

Tom Nevers Head

# NANTUCKET
*and Other New England*
# COOKING

by Arthur Hawkins
*The Steak Book*
*Who Needs a Cookbook*
*The Antisocial Cookbook*
*Cook It Quick*
*The Complete Seafood Cookbook*
*The Architectural Cookbook*
*Kids Cooking*
 (with Aileen Paul)
*Candies, Cakes and Cookies*
 (with Aileen Paul)

by Nancy Hawkins
*Let's Cook*

also by Nancy & Arthur Hawkins
*Chef's Special*
*Chef's Magic*
*The Low Cost Meat Book*
*The American Regional Cookbook*

# NANTUCKET
## *and Other New England*
# COOKING

NANCY & ARTHUR HAWKINS
& MARY ALLEN HAVEMEYER

*with*
*drawings by George Buctel*
*& Arthur Hawkins*

HASTINGS HOUSE, PUBLISHERS

NEW YORK

*To Mitch*

LIBRARY OF CONGRESS CATALOGING IN PUBLICATION DATA
Hawkins, Nancy.        Nantucket and other New England Cooking.
Includes index.
1. Cookery, American—New England.  I. Hawkins,
Arthur, joint author.  II. Havemeyer, Mary Allen,
joint author.  III. Title.
TX715.H3922        641.5'974        76-3523
ISBN 0-8038-5046-8

Published simultaneously in Canada by
Saunders of Toronto, Ltd., Don Mills, Ontario
*Printed in the United States of America*

# CONTENTS

# FOREWORD

This book was written by request.

There are other Nantucket cookbooks, some containing recipes collected from housewives and put together by church groups and clubs, and others compiled by cooking enthusiasts like ourselves, but none is quite complete in itself. The recipes in some are repeated, understandably, over and over again, and a considerable number are vague, imprecise and difficult to follow, calling for a "pinch" of this and a "handful" of that. Often no cooking time or oven temperature is specified.

So, an accumulation of demands for a definitive, all-inclusive book dealing with the best and most authentic foods of Nantucket and its immediate environs spurred the authors to a campaign of interviews with Island gastronomes. We set out to discover for ourselves what Nantucketers eat, how they cook it, and where they get their recipes. We sat and talked day after day with recent "transplants" and with islanders, some of whose families have been residents for several generations.

Many dictated to us their most cherished recipes and graciously lent us books and recipe collections passed down to them through the years, some written by hand on scraps of yellowing paper, and some so gray with age as to be almost unreadable.

We learned about the seasonal foods abundant in the sea waters, fresh waters and moors of Nantucket. We learned about clamming and scalloping and scupping and fishing for stripers, flounder and alewives; about picking cranberries and gathering beach plums, rose hips, fiddleheads and cattails. We learned about the Nantucket-born goose that returns home every year, about the wild ducks, quail and other game birds, and about the deer and rabbits that remain all year.

All the lore and all the native recipes we have been able to acquire, plus interesting recipes not so native, have gone into this book. We have given special attention to foods, natural and cultivated, indigenous to Nantucket, foods not usually stocked in the markets but available to those who desire to go out and get them—the berries, the game and the infinite variety of seafood.

We hope this is the cookbook you asked for.

# INTRODUCTION

Ishmael, the hero of *Moby-Dick*, exclaimed ecstatically after having eaten clam chowder on Nantucket Island. "Oh, sweet friends! hearken to me. It was made of sweet juicy clams, scarcely bigger than hazel nuts, mixed with pounded ship biscuit, and salted pork cut up in little flakes; the whole enriched with butter, and plentifully seasoned with pepper and salt." Ishmael and his friend Queequeg, a Kanaka from the South Sea Islands, found the chowder to be "surpassingly excellent" and so ordered Cod Chowder. Ishmael said, "In a few minutes the savory steam came forth again, but with a different flavor, and in good time a fine cod-chowder was placed before us." After a few days of this he was less enthusiastic when he said, "Fishiest of all fishy places was the Try Pots, which well deserved its name, for the pots there were always boiling chowders. Chowder for breakfast, and chowder for dinner, and chowder for supper, till you began to look for fish-bones coming through your clothes."

Fortunately the fare on the island was even then far broader than it was at the Try Pots. Among the clam recipes a delicious one is Quahaug Pie made of ground clams in piecrust, well seasoned with pepper and butter; another is what is called a "stifle." "A stifle is a chowder without water," said an island-born cook. The variety of shellfish and fish recipes comes from the plenitude of the Atlantic Ocean, Nantucket Sound and Harbor, where scallops are dug when the tide is low enough, and from the ingenuity of island cooks. Alewives, a kind of herring, are cooked and pickled in the spring when they are caught in the brooks and streams.

At first most foods were homegrown, milled and fished, except for coffee, sugar and spices. Sometimes supplies were brought by small trading sloops from Cape Cod. From the need to use everything have come such individual dishes as Brant's Pie (a cranberry raisin pie), Beach Plum Jelly, Rose Hip Jelly, Berry Pudding, Cranberry Dumplings, Breakfast Bannock, Whitpot, Soft Gingerbread, and Wonders. Quarter Peck Wedding Cake is a recipe dating from 1674. Shearing Buns, soft buttery buns leavened with yeast, were baked by the hundreds for sheepshearing days.

The Annual Sheepshearing was a big festival that lasted for two days. By the Quaker Calendar it fell on the second and third days nearest the twentieth of the sixth month. The animals were pastured in communal lands on the moors, a custom the first settlers had brought with them to the island when they escaped from their Puritan village and from the elders' wrath for having sheltered Quakers during a storm. The island Algonquian Indians taught them and introduced them to the "Squantum," an outdoor feast, and perhaps to a "Rantun Scoot," a sort of picnic with no preplanned destination. The summer shearing days were holidays. Coming in June when the weather was warm and balmy, even the sober Quakers were ready for a good time. Buns, cakes, Quahaug Pies, pickles and Wonders by the dozen were piled into picnic baskets and then into tipcarts, along with the family. Tents made of old sails were set up on the moors, and the fun began.

In the Nantucket household, "breakfast began with chowder, fried salt pork or fish, with potatoes, buckwheat cakes and molasses, topped off with wonders and pie." For those who believe chitlins belong only to southern Blacks, there is a famous Nantucket dish called Chitlins and Britches, served in the spring when the cod are running. Britches (breeches) are cod roe, and chitlins (chitterlings) are pigs' intestines.

Eleanor Early, author of *Island Patchwork,* tried to find a recipe for wonders. She advertised and received thirty-five responses, which turned out to be recipes for doughnuts. There was a difference. Wonders were cut oblong and scored with a jagger wheel made of whalebone or whittled from wood, then cooked in deep fat. She found them better than doughnuts, lighter and crunchier.

Corn pudding on Nantucket was a work of supreme cookery. Eleanor Early quotes Lucretia Mott, an islander and early pioneer in the emancipation of women, this way: "Much," she said, "depends on the corn. If the corn be young and milky, thee will not need so much milk, and thee must stiffen the mixture with eggs and crackers, and if the corn be old, thee must use more eggs. Judgement and experience are the best guides." She made it with "green corn," two dozen ears "well filled out."

The twelve wind and water mills on the Island produced meal for Bannock, Johnny Cake and a dish called Whitpot which is a version of Hasty Pudding. One wind mill is still grinding. Mendon Bannock is a spoon bread made with milk. Breakfast Bannock, less rich, is made with half water and half milk, and is simply baked in a pie tin. One tablespoon of sugar is used in Bannocks and Johnny Cake.

Quarter Peck Old Fashioned Wedding Cake was made with yeast and forty eggs, and wine. It was mixed and set between cushions to be sure it would rise overnight, and was baked in loaves. Mrs. Peter Foulger (or Folger—there was casual spelling in those days) is said to have baked this cake in 1674. She was a forbear of Benjamin Franklin's mother. Another curious custom in Nantucket was that of the Second Day Wedding given by the family of the groom. Anna Coffin baked a pudding for one of these; ever since, the recipe has been called Second Day Wedding Pudding. She served it with a brandy sauce, a shocking innovation for the abstemious folk. Her pudding was a raisin pudding. Most puddings were steamed in sailcloth.

In whaling days there was a custom that when a returning ship was sighted and its identity known, the captain's wife would hurry home and bake a large loaf of gingerbread to welcome him. There are five different recipes for gingerbread to be found in one cookbook, including comments about the virtues of each. It must have been a great favorite.

While the men were at sea, the women were busy running the family business and going to tea parties. These were also attended by whichever men were in port. Every afternoon tables were laid with goose, turkey, hams, puffs, wonders, Canton ginger and other good things from around the world. Tea was drunk from Chinese porcelain cups and, where earlier thrift had been the watchword, now no expense was spared. Voyages lasted up to five years and extended to the South Pacific and the China Seas. Whalers returned with whale oil, silks, satin, ivory, curries, Polynesian recipes, as well as coconuts, bananas and spices. They built beautiful Federal and Classic Revival houses that contrasted with the simple gray shingle homes of the Quaker village.

The last whaler left the harbor in 1869 and Nantucket went into a decline until discovered by vacationers. The men turned to cod fishing and went to Siasconset, Madaket and Wauwinet to fish. There was a saying that the cod jumped right out of the Harbor into the frying pan in Siasconset. S'conset is situated on a bluff above the sea. Fishermen built huts on the bluff. In the spring the catch was cod, in summer bluefish. Meals were cooked over wood fires. "There was a skillet for chowder, a spider for fish, and a kettle for tea, and a man, named Micah Coffin, hired an Indian to fish for him so that he could cook all day." The living was so pleasant wives came to visit and stayed. Slowly the little rose-covered houses grew and porches were built where food was cooked in bad weather. Kitchens are still called porches in S'conset as are all el-shaped kitchens, for that matter, on the Island.

More "strangers" came to the island. The Quaker power waned. "Strangers," as off-islanders are called, bought the beautiful old houses and cottages as vacation homes. Yachts instead of whalers plied the harbor and good quick meals were, and are, prepared in their galleys. Summer dinner parties are given where clever cooks use packaged and semipackaged foods to concoct *haute-cuisine* recipes, taking the least time to create great dinners. Other parties are catered by expert Island cooks. Box lunches are packed for picnickers. Real Portuguese bread is baked and sold. There are fine restaurants.

All these different strains are mixed together. The island-born still make chowder and Quahaug Pie and Cranberry Dumplings; the sailors make their fast tasty meals, and the vacationers make both. Homemade chowder can be bought frozen, and lobster is brought in from Maine and Nantucket waters. The Saturday tourist can eat any one of forty or more varieties of ice cream, and he can buy homemade beach-plum and rose-hip jellies in the shops. Altogether, the variety is scarcely believable for so small a piece of the globe.

# CHOWDERS
# & SOUPS

## NANTUCKET SCALLOP CHOWDER

| | |
|---|---|
| 2 cups diced potatoes | 1 teaspoon pepper |
| 1 cup clam broth | 6 sea crackers, toasted |
| 4 cups scalded milk | ¼ pound salt pork, diced |
| 1 pint bay scallops | 1 onion, thinly sliced |
| 1 teaspoon salt | 2 tablespoons butter |

Put potatoes, clam broth, milk, scallops, salt, pepper and crackers into a large pot or kettle.

Sauté the salt pork in a heavy skillet until crisp. Remove the cracklings and set aside. Leave fat in skillet.

Sauté the onion in the pork fat until brown. Add the onion and 1 tablespoon fat to the pot with potatoes and scallops.

Heat for 30 minutes, but do not boil. Stir in the butter and the pork cracklings, and serve.

*4 to 6 servings*                                          *quick*

# ROCKLAND FISHERMAN'S CHOWDER

This Down-East chowder is standard fare for the region. Cod, flounder, halibut—or any fish that's running at the time—may be substituted for the haddock. Note that the potatoes are sliced both thick and thin; the thin slices cook up and form the thickener, a custom probably borrowed from the method of cooking Irish stew.

6 tablespoons butter, or 2 ounces salt pork, diced
12 small white onions, or 3 medium-size onions, cubed
6 medium-size potatoes, peeled
2 teaspoons salt
1 teaspoon pepper
1 teaspoon dried thyme
2 cups hot water
1½ pounds haddock fillets, fresh or frozen
1 quart milk, scalded
1 cup half-and-half

Melt 3 tablespoons butter in a heavy pot, put in the onions, and sauté until golden.

Cut 3 potatoes into thick slices and 3 potatoes into very thin slices. Add these, the seasonings and the hot water to the pot, and simmer until the thin potatoes cook up.

Place the fillets on top, cover, and simmer for 10 minutes.

Add the milk and half-and-half. Reheat and serve.

*4 to 6 servings*                                              *quick*

## CAPE COD OYSTER CHOWDER

2 ounces salt pork, diced
1 cup minced onion
2 cups thinly sliced potatoes
2 dozen shucked oysters with
    liquor
2 cups milk

2 cups light cream
2 tablespoons butter
¼ teaspoon dried thyme
1 teaspoon salt
½ teaspoon freshly ground
    pepper

Sauté the salt pork in a large pot or kettle until crisp. Remove cracklings and reserve, leaving fat in the kettle.

Add the onion to the kettle and sauté for 5 minutes; do not brown.

Return the pork cracklings to the kettle; add the potatoes, oyster liquor and enough water to cover. Simmer for 20 minutes, or until potatoes are tender.

Add the milk, cream, butter, seasonings and oysters. Simmer over low heat until the edges of the oysters curl. Serve hot with oyster crackers.

*4 to 6 servings*                                        *quick*

---

## NEW ENGLAND QUAHAUG CHOWDER

¼ pound salt pork, diced
4 medium-size onions, chopped
1 cup clam broth
2 cups diced potatoes
1 quart milk
3 cups ground or chopped
    quahaugs

1 teaspoon salt
1 teaspoon pepper
½ cup flour mixed with 2
    tablespoons melted
    butter
thyme

Brown the salt pork in a large pot or kettle until crisp and nutty. Add the onions and sauté until golden.

Add the clam broth, potatoes, milk, quahaugs, seasonings and butter-flour mixture. Cook without boiling for 15 minutes, or until potatoes are softened.

Serve in soup bowls with crackers and a shaker of dried thyme on the table.

*4 to 6 servings*                                        *quick*

## CHICKEN CHOWDER

1 fowl, 4 to 5 pounds, cut up
¼ pound salt pork, diced
2 medium-size onions, diced

6 medium-size potatoes, sliced
fresh thyme, chopped

Simmer fowl in water to cover for 2 to 3 hours. Keep water level above chicken.

Fry out pork dice; remove the pork cracklings from skillet and reserve. Leave fat in skillet. Add the onions, potatoes and 2 cups broth from the chicken to the skillet. Cook until potatoes are just tender, about 10 minutes.

Skim fat from pot of simmering chicken. Add onion and potato mixture. Let simmer for a few minutes longer.

Serve in soup bowls, a piece of chicken in the center and potatoes around. Sprinkle with fresh thyme and salt-pork cracklings.

*6 to 8 servings*

---

## CORN CHOWDER

1 small onion, sliced
3 tablespoons butter
4 potatoes, diced
2 cups water
2 cups fresh, frozen or
    canned corn

4 cups milk
1 teaspoon salt
½ teaspoon pepper

Sauté the onion in the butter in a large pot until golden. Add the potatoes and water and cook until potatoes are softened.

Add corn, milk, salt and pepper. Heat for 10 minutes, but do not boil.

*6 servings*                                        *quick*

# CREAM OF ASPARAGUS SOUP

1 pound fresh asparagus, or
    1 package (10 ounces)
      frozen
1 tablespoon chopped onion
2 cups chicken broth

2 tablespoons butter
2 tablespoons flour
2 cups milk, scalded
salt and pepper
butter

Cook the asparagus in a heavy saucepan with just enough water to cover until soft. Remove asparagus from liquid, and cut off and reserve tips. Leave cooking liquid in the pot.

Purée asparagus stems in blender, and return to pot. Add the onion and chicken broth, and simmer for 5 minutes.

Melt the butter in a small skillet, stir in the flour until smooth, and add to the soup. Add the scalded milk, and season to taste.

Add the reserved asparagus tips and a dab of butter to each bowl.

*4 servings*                                           *quick*

---

# BOSTON BAKED BEAN SOUP

1 cup baked beans
1 cup chopped celery
1 cup chopped onion
½ cup fresh or canned
    tomatoes

3 cups consommé
1 teaspoon salt
½ teaspoon pepper

Put the beans, celery, onion and tomatoes into a heavy pot, and simmer for 30 minutes.

Put through a sieve or food mill and add the consommé. Heat, season, and serve.

*4 servings*                                           *quick*

## MAINE CABBAGE SOUP

¼ cup water
½ medium-size head of fresh
  cabbage, shredded
1 large potato, peeled and
  thinly sliced
1 large onion, peeled and
  thinly sliced

3 cups milk
4 tablespoons butter
1 teaspoon salt
¼ teaspoon pepper
grated mild cheese

Put ¼ cup water in a heavy saucepan; add cabbage, potato and onion. Stir, cover tightly, and cook over low heat until vegetables are very tender. Then mash with a potato masher into a pulp.

Add the milk, butter, salt and pepper; stir. Keep hot, but do not boil. Serve in bowls, with grated cheese on top.

*4 servings*

## CRANBERRY SOUP

½ cup chopped shallots or
  spring onions
1 tablespoon butter
1 can (1 pound) beets with
  juice, chopped
1 pound cranberries

3 cups chicken broth
¼ cup sherry
1 teaspoon salt
½ teaspoon pepper
lemon slices

Sauté the shallots in the butter for a few minutes, or until soft, and transfer to a blender container.

Add the beets with juice and blend until puréed. Transfer to a bowl.

Simmer the cranberries in the broth for 5 minutes, or until berries pop. Pour into blender container and purée. Put through a sieve and add to the puréed beets.

Flavor with sherry, season with salt and pepper, and serve hot or cold garnished with lemon slices.

*6 servings*                                                    *quick*

# PORTUGUESE KALE SOUP

1 pound salt pork
1 onion, chopped
3 leeks, cut into 1-inch pieces
8 cups water
3 cups kale leaves
6 carrots, cut into 1-inch
    pieces

6 potatoes, peeled and
    quartered
½ teaspoon salt
¼ teaspoon pepper

Wash salt pork, and trim if necessary. Put in a large kettle, and add onion, leeks and water. Bring to a boil.

Strip leaves from kale stems, and chop leaves. Add to soup, with carrots and potatoes. Add seasonings and simmer for 1½ hours.

Serve in soup plates with a slice of salt pork in each. Accompany with rye bread or pumpernickel.

*4 to 6 servings*

# STONINGTON LOBSTER BISQUE

3 tablespoons butter
1 tablespoon minced onion
1 teaspoon minced parsley
2 tablespoons flour
½ teaspoon dried thyme
1 teaspoon salt
¼ teaspoon pepper

few grains of cayenne
1½ cups minced freshly
    cooked lobster meat
2 cups chicken broth
2 cups light cream
½ cup sherry

Melt the butter in a heavy pot; stir in the onion and parsley. Cook slowly until onion is light brown.

Stir in the flour until mixture thickens. Add the seasonings and lobster meat and cook for 5 minutes, stirring. Stir in the broth and cook for 15 minutes longer.

Remove from the heat, stir in the cream and sherry, and serve in cups.

*6 servings* *quick*

# OYSTER OR CLAM STEW

This is a sort of all-purpose recipe for seafood stews. The method can be used for making scallop, shrimp or lobster stew simply by substituting these shellfish for oysters or clams.

| | |
|---|---|
| 2 tablespoons butter | 2 dozen shucked oysters or |
| 2 cups milk | Cherrystone clams with |
| 2 cups light cream | broth |
| 1 teaspoon salt | butter |
| ½ teaspoon celery seeds | minced parsley |
| ½ teaspoon pepper | |

Put the butter, milk, cream and seasonings into a heavy pot with the oyster liquor or clam broth. Bring to a simmer and cook for 2 minutes.

Add the oysters or clams and cook for 3 minutes longer.

Serve in bowls, garnished with a dab of butter and parsley.

*4 servings*                                                                 *quick*

---

*Capt. Stephen Bailey, partaking of an oyster stew at a church supper, called the waitress with, "See here, my lass, can't ye get me some more oysters? These here are a day's sail apart."*

---

## NEW ENGLAND ONION SOUP

| | |
|---|---|
| 2 tablespoons butter | ½ teaspoon freshly ground |
| 4 large onions, thinly sliced | pepper |
| 2 tablespoons flour | ½ teaspoon grated mace |
| 2 cups milk | 2 egg yolks |
| 2 cups chicken broth | ½ cup heavy cream |
| 1 teaspoon salt | minced parsley |

Melt the butter in a large pot or kettle, add the onions, and cook until transparent but not brown.

Stir in the flour until well blended. Gradually add the milk, stirring until smooth, then stir in the broth. Add the seasonings and simmer for 5 minutes.

Beat the egg yolks with the cream and pour into a soup tureen. Gradually stir in the soup. Sprinkle with minced parsley and serve.

*4 to 6 servings*

## SPLIT-PEA SOUP

Lima-bean soup or lentil soup may be made by following this same recipe. Lentils cook more quickly. Lentil soup is often served with slices of cooked frankfurters floating in the bowl.

| | |
|---|---|
| 2 cups dried split peas | ¼ cup chopped parsley |
| 1 quart water | pinch of dried thyme |
| 1 ham bone, or 2-inch cube | 1 bay leaf |
| of salt pork, scored | 1 teaspoon salt |
| 1 onion, sliced | 1 teaspoon pepper |
| 1 celery rib | hot milk |

Put the peas into a large pot or kettle with 1 quart water, the ham bone or salt pork, the onion, celery, parsley and seasonings. Cover and simmer for 2 hours, or until peas are soft.

Remove and discard the celery and ham bone, and put soup through a sieve.

Dilute to desired consistency with hot milk, and serve with croutons.

*4 to 6 servings*

## VERY SPECIAL SCALLOP SOUP

2 medium-size carrots,
  chopped
2 medium-size onions,
  chopped
2 celery ribs, chopped
1 bay leaf
3 tablespoons chopped
  parsley
½ teaspoon freshly ground
  pepper, or a few
  peppercorns

1 cup clam juice, fresh or
  canned
2 cups dry white wine
1 cup water
16 to 20 bay scallops, or 8 sea
  scallops, coarsely
  chopped
chopped chives

Simmer the vegetables and seasonings in the liquids for 1 hour.

Put the mixture through a sieve, and return the liquid to the pot.

At 4 or 5 minutes before serving, add the scallops, simmer for a
few minutes, and serve topped with chopped chives.

*4 servings*

## MADAKET CURRIED SCALLOP SOUP

1½ pounds bay scallops
2 cups fish stock or clam
  broth
1 small onion, minced
1 garlic clove, minced
1 tablespoon curry powder

½ teaspoon dried thyme
½ teaspoon freshly ground
  pepper
½ cup heavy cream
2 tablespoons dry sherry

Simmer scallops in the stock for 5 minutes. Remove scallops from
liquid and set aside.

Add the onion, garlic and seasonings to the stock and simmer for
10 minutes.

Return the scallops, and add cream and sherry. Heat, but do not
boil. Serve hot or cold.

*4 servings*                                                    *quick*

## SCUP BISQUE

2 pounds scup fillets
3 tablespoons butter
1 teaspoon chopped onion
2 tablespoons chopped celery
2 tablespoons chopped
    mushrooms
1 teaspoon salt

½ teaspoon freshly ground
    pepper
2 tablespoons flour
2 cups chicken broth
1 cup light cream
2 tablespoons dry sherry

Simmer the scup in salted water until soft. Drain; discard cooking water. Flake the flesh with a fork and set aside.

Melt the butter in a heavy pot, and stir in the onion, celery, mushrooms and seasonings.

Stir in the flour, then the broth, and cook until smooth and thickened.

Add the scup flakes, stir, and remove from the heat. Stir in the cream and sherry, and serve.

*4 to 6 servings*

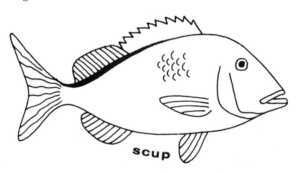

scup

## CREAM OF WATERCRESS SOUP

1 bunch of watercress,
   minced
2 cups chicken broth
2 tablespoons butter
2 tablespoons flour

1 cup light cream
1 teaspoon salt
½ teaspoon pepper
few grains of cayenne

Simmer the watercress in the broth for 10 minutes. Purée everything in an electric blender or force through a sieve.

Melt the butter in a small skillet, stir in the flour until smooth, and add to the purée. Heat and stir until well blended.

Remove from the heat, stir in the cream and seasonings, and serve in cups.

*4 servings*     *quick*

## CREAM OF WHITE TURNIP SOUP

1 Nantucket white turnip,
   about 1 pound
1 teaspoon salt

3 cups milk
3 tablespoons butter
3 tablespoons flour

Peel and cut up turnip, put in water to cover, and cook for about 20 minutes, or until tender. Mash in the pot, or put through a food mill. Add salt.

Heat milk and add to turnip. Mix butter and flour into a roux and stir into soup until thick. Serve.

*4 to 6 servings*

Finally, here are two recipes for a soup that no definitive New England cookbook should be without. Nantucketers, without exception, serve Whale Chowder every St. Vitus' Day. The children happily dance around the pot, dipping their spoons into the delectable broth, as the chowder cooks, while the old folk sit and sip blubber cocktails.

## NANTUCKET WHALE CHOWDER I

This is a famous old Nantucket dish dating from the days when the island was an important whaling port. The recipe, scrawled upon a fragment of yellowed-with-age parchment, was discovered among the effects of old Captain Foggerty, who was a frequent visitor to Nantucket.

1 whale, skinned, eviscerated
    and with blubber and tail
    removed
½ pound salt pork, chopped
1 garlic clove, minced
4 large potatoes, peeled and
    diced
4 large onions, chopped

4 celery ribs, chopped
1 bay leaf
pinch of grated mace
1 teaspoon salt
½ teaspoon pepper
2 quarts hot water (Captain
    Foggerty used rum)

Remove the breast meat from the whale, discarding the wings, thighs and fins (or reserve them for subsequent use).

Try out the salt pork in a heavy pot, add the garlic, and cook for 2 minutes.

Add the vegetables, seasonings and liquid. Simmer for 10 minutes.

Dice the whale breast and add 3 cups to the pot, discarding the remainder (or you can reserve it for subsequent use).

Simmer for 4 to 6 hours, or until whale is tender, adding additional liquid as needed. Serve garnished with minced quince.

*serves 4 comfortably*

# NANTUCKET WHALE CHOWDER II

The following modern-day recipe was contributed by a Nantucketer who, never having seen a whale let alone cooked one, nevertheless has spent a great deal of time in the Whaling Museum. We give you the recipe exactly as it was written.

PREPARING:

You'll need one *small* whale. While you may have to pay your seafood market as much as $50 to $60 a ton more, it will be worth it—no leftover problems.

Borrow cutting tools from your friendly whaling museum in exchange for skeleton. Remove blubber in conventional way and sell it to whaling museum. (We've never seen one with fresh blubber on exhibit.)

To remove meat use freshly sharpened chain saw, being careful to avoid damage to skeleton. Phone whaling museum and have them remove the skeleton and blubber immediately.

Cut meat into small bite-size pieces. Time required for this varies, but the usual rule of thumb is to allow 12 or 13 man hours per ton.

COOKING:

Put meat into a large pot or boiler and barely cover with fresh water. Then add 1 or 2 pinches of salt. (There's a great deal of controversy about this; we belong to the 2-pinch school of thought.) Light fire beneath pot and stir. Next day your chowder should start to boil. As water level lowers, replace with heavy cream. (For a whale originally weighing 20 tons you will only need about 60 gallons.) Continue stirring for 36 hours.

Now is the time for the gourmet touches. You will need potatoes, onions, salt pork and such seasonings as cayenne, bay leaves, celery and so on. As to quantity, check your favorite chowder recipe. If you've had success with 10 onions per gallon, it is obvious that you will need 10,000 for each 1,000 gallons of whale chowder. When the stirring watch isn't looking, we always sneak in 2 more pinches of salt hidden in a bay leaf.

Depending on size of whale this will serve 1800 to 2200 people.

Humor aside, whale meat is eaten in many parts of the world, much to the distress of environmentalists. The herds have been seriously depleted, enough to make the once plentiful whale an endangered species. The following quote shows that it was not disdained as food by early Nantucketers.

*"Whale was occasionally eaten [on whaling ships] and porpoise meat, and sometimes fresh fish found a place on the festive board; and when they were trying out, advantage was taken of the abundance of hot fat to do more or less frying in the trypots."* Quaint Nantucket, *William Root Bliss*

# EGGS, CHEESES
# & PASTA

## NANTUCKET BAKED OMELET

6 eggs, separated
2 cups plus 2 tablespoons
   milk
2 tablespoons butter

⅛ teaspoon pepper
1 teaspoon salt
1 teaspoon flour

Preheat oven to 350° F.

Beat egg yolks. Beat egg whites until stiff.

Heat 2 cups milk and the butter, but do not boil.

Mix together pepper, salt, flour, and 2 tablespoons cold milk. Stir into the hot milk, then add slowly to the egg yolks. Fold in the egg whites.

Pour into a buttered baking dish and bake until set like baked custard. Serve in the baking dish.

*4 to 6 servings*                                                                 *quick*

---

## POTATO OMELET

2 tablespoons bacon fat
1½ cups cubed peeled
   potatoes
1 onion, thinly sliced
1 teaspoon salt

¼ teaspoon pepper
4 eggs
3 tablespoons water
2 tablespoons butter

Heat bacon fat in a heavy skillet, add potatoes and onion, and cook and turn until potatoes are brown. Season with ½ teaspoon salt and ⅛ teaspoon pepper. Reduce heat.

Beat together eggs, water, remaining salt and pepper.

Melt butter over low heat in another skillet and pour in the eggs. Stir until beginning to set. Spread potato mixture over the omelet. Fold over, and turn onto a hot platter. Serve with chili sauce.

*4 servings* *quick*

## HOT DEVILED EGGS ON TOAST

8 eggs, hard cooked
2 tablespoons mayonnaise
1 teaspoon prepared mustard
½ teaspoon salt

⅛ teaspoon pepper
4 slices of buttered toast
paprika

Carefully cut the eggs into halves and remove the yolks. Save the white halves.

Mash yolks, add mayonnaise, mustard, salt and pepper, and mash well together. Pile into the white halves.

Put 4 egg halves on each piece of toast. Sprinkle with paprika, and serve.

*4 servings*

## BAKED EGGS

4 tablespoons butter
8 eggs
½ teaspoon salt

⅛ teaspoon pepper
4 rashers of bacon (optional)

Preheat oven to 400° F.

Divide butter among 4 individual ramekins, and melt in oven.

Break 2 eggs into each ramekin. Return dishes to oven and cook for 10 minutes, or until eggs are set. Sprinkle with seasoning.

A rasher of bacon can be put across each dish while cooking. Turn bacon after 5 minutes.

*4 servings* *quick*

## POACHED EGGS AND HADDOCK

| | |
|---|---|
| 1 smoked haddock | 4 tablespoons melted butter |
| 6 cups water | 4 lemon slices |
| 4 eggs | |

Cover haddock with 2 cups water and bring to a boil. Drain at once. Remove skin and bones, and divide haddock into 4 pieces. Keep hot.

Bring 4 cups water to a simmer. Break each egg and slide it into simmering water. Poach until whites are cooked.

Put 1 piece of fish on each plate. Cover each with a well-drained poached egg, and top with 1 tablespoon melted butter. Put 1 lemon slice on each serving.

*4 servings* *quick*

## SCOTCH EGGS

| | |
|---|---|
| 4 eggs, hard cooked | bread crumbs |
| 1 pound sausage meat | 2 cups lard |
| 1 uncooked egg, beaten | |

Shell hard-cooked eggs and cover each all around with sausage meat.

Roll in beaten egg and bread crumbs and fry in lard heated to 360° F. until sausage meat is cooked.

Cut each egg into halves, and serve.

*4 servings* *quick*

## EGG AND BACON PIE

4 eggs
2 cups milk
½ teaspoon salt
⅛ teaspoon pepper

pastry for 2-crust, 9-inch pie,
  unbaked (p. 172)
4 rashers of bacon, cooked
  rare

Preheat oven to 375° F.

Mix eggs, milk, salt and pepper.

Put half of pastry in a pie pan; put bacon slices on pastry. Pour in the custard. Cover with remaining pastry. Crimp edges.

Bake for 10 minutes. Reduce heat to 300° F., and bake for 35 to 40 minutes more, until custard is set.

Serve hot or cold.

*6 servings*

## RINKTUM TIDDY

This is a quick supper or lunch dish, traditional in early New England days.

1 tablespoon butter
1 small onion, finely chopped
2 cups chopped fresh
  tomatoes
1 teaspoon salt
¼ teaspoon pepper

2 teaspoons sugar
½ pound American cheese,
  grated
1 egg, beaten
4 pieces of toast, buttered

Melt butter; add onion, tomatoes, salt, pepper and sugar. Cook for 5 minutes.

Add cheese and cook, stirring, until melted. Remove from heat and stir in the egg.

Spoon evenly onto slices of toast, and serve immediately.

*4 servings*                                                    *quick*

# HAM AND CHEESE CROQUETTES

Cut into smaller pieces, this makes an excellent hors d'oeuvre or cocktail snack.

3 tablespoons butter
3 tablespoons flour
¾ cup milk
2 egg yolks, beaten
1 cup diced sharp American
    cheese

½ cup chopped ham
½ cup bread crumbs
butter for frying

Melt butter, stir in flour, and stir in milk gradually until thickened. Remove from heat.

Stir in egg yolks, cheese and ham until cheese is melted. Pour into a dish and cool.

Cut into strips 2 by 3 inches. Dip into bread crumbs and fry quickly in butter. Drain on paper towel and keep hot. Serve immediately.

*6 servings*                                                    *quick*

---

# SPAGHETTI WITH WHITE CLAM SAUCE

1 teaspoon salt
5 tablespoons olive oil
30 Little Neck clams, shucked
3 garlic cloves, finely chopped

3 tablespoons chopped
    parsley
1 pound spaghetti

Fill a 4-quart pot with water and bring to a boil. Add salt and 1 tablespoon oil. In the meantime, chop the clams and reserve the juice.

Put remaining oil in a saucepan and sauté the garlic and parsley until golden. Add clam juice and simmer gently.

Add spahetti to boiling water. Wait until pasta sinks, then stir to separate strands. Boil rapidly for 12 to 15 minutes, until just cooked through. Drain and keep in pot.

Add chopped clams to garlic sauce and cook for 3 minutes. Stir into spaghetti. Serve with Italian bread and a salad.

*4 to 6 servings*                                               *quick*

## MACARONI, MASSACHUSETTS STYLE

2 cups elbow macaroni
2 quarts water, boiling
½ pound chipped beef
2 tablespoons butter

3 tablespoons flour
2 cups milk
¼ cup cracker crumbs

Drop macaroni into boiling water and cook for 15 to 20 minutes; drain.

Soak chipped beef in water to cover for 10 minutes; drain. Mix with the macaroni and put into buttered 1½-quart baking dish.

Melt butter over low heat, stir in flour, add milk gradually, and stir until the sauce thickens. Pour over macaroni. (2 cups milk can be used instead of sauce.)

Preheat oven to 375° F.

Spread crumbs over top of dish, and bake for 15 to 20 minutes, until crumbs are brown.

*6 servings*

## NOODLES WITH ZUCCHINI MEAT SAUCE

4 quarts water
2 tablespoons olive oil
3 tablespoons butter
2 tablespoons minced onion
1 tablespoon minced carrot
1 tablespoon minced parsley
1 pound meat, chopped
1 tomato, chopped

1 zucchini, peeled and cut
    into ½-inch-thick
    crosswise slices
2 teaspoons salt
1 garlic clove
1 pound noodles
½ cup grated Parmesan
    cheese

Bring 4 quarts of water to a boil.

Put olive oil in a saucepan with 1 tablespoon butter. Sauté onion, carrot and parsley in butter until just golden. Add meat, piece by piece, and stir and cook until all the pink is gone and meat begins to brown.

Add tomato, zucchini slices, 1 teaspoon salt and the whole garlic clove. Simmer for 5 to 10 minutes.

Put noodles in boiling water with remaining 1 teaspoon salt, and cook for 10 to 12 minutes. Drain.

Mix noodles with 2 tablespoons butter and half the cheese. Add sauce and mix. Serve with remaining Parmesan sprinkled over each serving.

*4 to 6 servings*

# SHELLFISH
# & FISH

*From a sea journal written in 1753 by a young man most interested in food: His name was Peleg Folger, perhaps a cousin of Benjamin Franklin.*

June 26th. We are in health & and so oyly yt we are in a Dole Pickle (ut aiunt) (as they say). We had a haglet stewpye for supper; about 8 at night we finished trying out our Blubber & put out the fire of our caboose. We sandrove our oyl and stowed it away in the hold, & and quoined it; our Whale made 68 barrels.

June 30th. This day we had corn'd fish for dinner. Pancakes for supper & and chocolate for Breakfast, the sea a little chopling and we lay under a trysail.

July 2d. We lay to all this 24 hours under trysail & drove to the Northward. The sea broke like surfe & and appear'd like a snowdrift. And we ship'd many tuns of water; . . . Our quarter deck was sometimes anckle deep & our tub of gravel got stove to pieces so we shall be forced to kill our fowl for fear they'l die. We had pancakes for supper. Lat. 60-30.

July 14th. We spoke with a ship from Glasgow. Elisha came on board of us & we had a fowl stewpye and a great plum pudding for dinner. Then we spyed whales & and we killed one large spermaceti & we got her alongside & began to cut her up.

From insurance office, Marine Journal:

Sunday October 13th (1804) Wind in the morning southerly with rain, then cleared up and hauled around to the westward. Sailed from the Bar the ship Rose for Canton.

The Rose sailed on her second voyage to China, laden with general merchandise, Spanish dollars, and shark fins for Chinese epicures.

# CLAMS

There are many types of clams lying around in the shallow waters of the world, but two species lead the field: the quahaugs, or hard clams (called chowders, Cherrystones, or Little Necks, depending upon age and size) and the mananose (soft clams or steamers).

Hard clams, or quahaugs, are in plentiful supply all along the New England coast. They are taken commercially by dredging and raking, but a way to get them yourself is to use an ordinary potato hoe—or go toeing for them. You wade around in shallow, sandy water, wiggling your toes until they make contact. On a good day and in a good spot, you can fill a pail in almost no time.

Soft clams, found almost anywhere there is sand on both sides of the Atlantic, bury themselves but maintain contact with the world by the necklike siphons; these, of course, give away their hiding place during low tide.

The variety of clams is almost infinite. The Pacific coast boasts of the bean clam, horse clam, butter clam, geoduck, pepitona and Pismo. Along the New England coast you can find, in addition to Little Necks, Cherrystones and chowders, the large seaclams sometimes called surf clams, bar clams or skimmers, the razor clams and the sunrays—all edible and nutritious.

## SCALLOPED CLAMS, NANTUCKET STYLE

2 cups minced Cherrystones          ¼ cup melted butter
  or Little Necks, with juice     ½ teaspoon pepper
1 cup cracker crumbs                 1 egg, beaten
1 cup milk or half-and-half

Mix all the ingredients together and let stand for 30 minutes.

Preheat oven to 350° F.

Transfer to a buttered casserole and bake for 45 minutes.

*4 servings*

## QUAHAUG BEER FRITTERS

2 cups flour                         1 cup beer
1 teaspoon baking powder             1 pint fresh quahaugs,
2 eggs, beaten                         minced, with juice
dash of Tabasco                      bacon fat or cooking oil

Sift together flour and baking powder. Stir in the eggs, Tabasco and beer to make a smooth batter.

Stir in the minced clams. Drop by tablespoons onto a hot greased griddle. Cook for about 6 minutes on each side, or until golden.

*6 servings*                                                    *quick*

## NEW BEDFORD QUAHAUG PATTIES

2 cups ground or chopped             ¾ cup cracker crumbs
  quahaugs with juice            1 teaspoon paprika
2 eggs, well beaten                  1 teaspoon salt

Mix together the quahaugs, beaten eggs, cracker crumbs and seasonings.

Drop by tablespoons onto a hot greased griddle, and cook for about 4 minutes on each side, or until golden brown.

*4 servings*                                                    *quick*

# NANTUCKET QUAHAUG PIE

The Indians called them *pourquois,* New Yorkers call them *chowder clams.* Call them what you will, quahaugs are as indispensable to Nantucket as beans are to Boston. This pie, incidentally, should be made without salt, since the clams themselves are sufficiently salty.

6 to 8 large quahaugs
pastry for 2-crust, 9-inch pie,
    unbaked (p. 172)
1½ teaspoons freshly ground
    pepper

3 tablespoons butter
2 tablespoons flour

Preheat oven to 350° F.

Remove quahaugs from their shells, grind, and drain, retaining juice.

Line a pie pan with half of the pastry, and fill with the ground clams. Sprinkle with pepper. Cover with the remaining pastry, pinch edges together, and puncture top with air vents. Bake until crust is golden.

Heat the clam juice and thicken with a roux made by combining the butter and flour. Serve sauce on the side.

*4 servings*

## CAPE COD CLAM PIE

1 quart Cherrystone or Little
    Neck clams
2 medium-size potatoes,
    peeled and thinly sliced
2 medium-size onions, thinly
    sliced

2 tablespoons melted butter
1 cup light cream
½ teaspoon pepper
pastry for 1-crust, deep-dish
    pie, unbaked (p. 172)

Preheat oven to 450° F.

Chop clams; retain the broth to use in the pie.

Put the clams, potatoes and onions into a 2-quart casserole in layers. Add the reserved broth, butter, cream and pepper.

Cover with the pastry, perforate with steam vents, and bake for about 30 minutes, or until crust is browned.

*4 servings*

---

## STUFFED QUAHAUGS

1 dozen medium-size
    quahaugs, scrubbed
1 onion, minced
½ garlic clove, minced
2-inch-square piece of salt
    pork ¼ inch thick, finely
    chopped

dash of pepper
dash of Tabasco
dash of Worcestershire sauce
½ cup cracker crumbs
1 egg, lightly beaten

Preheat oven to 350° F.

Steam the quahaugs open, or open by hand, but leave the shells hinged.

Drain juice into a bowl, add the quahaugs, and mince. Add the minced onion and garlic, chopped salt pork and seasonings.

Soak the cracker crumbs in a little quahaug juice, squeeze out, and add crumbs and the egg to the bowl.

Mix thoroughly, and stuff into the hinged shells. Close shells and tie tightly. Place in a shallow pan and bake for about 45 minutes.

*4 to 6 servings*

## STEAMED SOFT CLAMS

A clam steamer is a double-compartmented cooker; the top part, where the clams go, is perforated. The bottom compartment, usually with a spigot for running off broth, contains a little water which, when heated, steams up into the top compartment to cook the clams. The process is simple and can be accomplished with makeshift utensils such as a pot of suitable size, a colander and a lid to hold in the steam.

To eat soft clams, first dip them into broth to remove any sand that may be present, and then dip into melted butter. When serving, allow at least a dozen per person.

*quick*

## NANTUCKET CLAMBAKE

When summer comes and the Nantucket weather becomes mild and enjoyable, good people get together and cook up an old-fashioned clambake on one of the many beaches. Down through the years there have always been a chosen few well known for their skill as *bake masters,* and one of these is called in to take charge.

The clambake may be under the auspices of a college group celebrating a class reunion, a club, or simply a group of dedicated old-timers. The procedure in Nantucket is pretty much as it is elsewhere in New England, with the ingredients varying according to the season and supply.

Here's how to do a clambake:

1. Dig a large hole in the sand and line it with rocks.
2. Build a fine, hot fire and lay on more large rocks.
3. When the rocks are good and hot, and the fire has died out, cover rocks with a layer of seaweed.
4. Add 6 live lobsters and another layer of seaweed.
5. Now, add 6 or 8 dozen scrubbed Cherrystone clams or steamers, wrapped in cheesecloth, and a thick layer of seaweed.

6. Add a dozen ears of corn, unshucked but with silk re-moved, and 6 sweet potatoes in foil.
7. Cover with a canvas tarpaulin, weighted with rocks and banked with sand around the edges. Bake for 2 or 3 hours, or until clams begin to open.

Serve with plenty of beer.

*6 servings*

## CLAMBAKE, LANDLUBBER STYLE

Just because you don't have a sandy beach to dig into, or because you don't wish to build a fire and heat up rocks, that's no reason for not having a clambake. The following washboiler method will work just as well and is a lot quicker.

1. Cover the bottom of a washboiler or large enamelware pot with clean seaweed, add a quart of water, and place over high heat.
2. When water boils add 2 chickens, quartered, each part wrapped in cheesecloth, and a layer of seaweed. Cover.
3. After 15 minutes add 4 lobsters, 1½ pounds each, and another layer of seaweed. Cover.
4. After 7 more minutes add 8 ears of corn, unhusked with silk removed, or each ear wrapped in foil, and another layer of seaweed. Cover.
5. After 10 more minutes add 6 dozen steamer clams wrapped in cheesecloth. Cover with lid or tarp and steam until clams open.

Cut the lobsters lengthwise into halves and serve the whole mess with melted butter and the kettle liquid as a dip.

*8 servings*

# BAKED QUAHAUGS

50 quahaugs
¼ pound salt pork

cracker crumbs

Preheat oven to 325° F.

Scrub clam shells well.

Grind clams and salt pork together. Mix in cracker crumbs. Fill scrubbed clam shells, cover with a second shell, and tie.

Bake for 20 minutes.

*16 to 24 servings*

# QUAHAUG STIFLE

1 quart shucked quahaugs
   with juice
¼ pound salt pork, diced
6 potatoes, peeled and sliced
1 onion, chopped

4 tablespoons butter, cut into
   pieces
½ teaspoon salt
⅛ teaspoon pepper

Cut soft bellies from quahaugs and chop remaining muscle. Strain juice.

Fry out salt-pork dice in a heavy pot over medium-low heat. Remove and reserve cracklings. Leave fat in pot.

Add sliced potatoes to hot fat. Add onion and strained clam juice. Cover skillet tightly, reduce heat, and cook for 10 minutes.

Spread clams and butter pieces over all. Cook for 10 minutes more. Sprinkle with salt and pepper. Spread cracklings over all and serve from pot with a shaker of thyme and common crackers.

Fillets or chunks of fish can be cooked on top of the potatoes instead of clams.

*6 servings*

*"Eel Stifle, like chowder only no milk, just salt pork, potatoes and eels."*

# SCALLOPS

Scallops, like oysters and clams, live between two shells. But unlike their cousins, scallops have the ability to move about in the water or on the sand by exercising the large muscle to open and close the shells. The entire scallop is edible, but in the United States only this muscle is eaten. Europeans eat the coral (or roe) as well.

Bay or cape scallops, only ½ inch thick, are sweeter and more tender than deep-sea scallops but are in season commercially only from November to April. During those months the bays and harbors of Nantucket are literally jammed with scallop boats, making scalloping the number one fishing industry of the island. The little scallop shacks that line the shores of Nantucket Bay are busy, as scallop openers are at work proving how fast they can flick a knife.

The month of October is reserved for family scalloping only. Attired in any old clothes and waders and armed with rakes and pushers and viewers (like divers' face masks), Nantucketers go forth into the shallow waters, towing along bushel baskets affixed to inner tubes for flotation. The bushel basket is the limit—quickly reached if a productive bed is discovered.

## SCALLOPS IN SHELL

| | |
|---|---|
| 2 cups bay scallops, or sea scallops cut up | 3 tablespoons flour |
| | 1 cup half-and-half |
| 6 tablespoons butter | 2 tablespoons sherry |
| 1½ teaspoons salt | dry bread crumbs |
| ½ teaspoon white pepper | paprika |
| 1 onion, minced | 1 lemon, quartered |

Sauté the scallops in 2 tablespoons butter for not more than 2 minutes, shaking the pan to cook on all sides. Season with 1 teaspoon salt and the pepper and transfer to 4 buttered scallop shells.

Preheat oven to 250° F.

Sauté the onion in 2 more tablespoons butter until just golden. Stir in the flour and then the half-and-half until mixture thickens.

Stir in the sherry, season with ½ teaspoon salt, and spoon sauce over the scallops.

Sprinkle with bread crumbs and paprika, dot with remaining butter, and place in oven until just golden. Serve with lemon wedges.

*4 servings*

## BAKED BAYS, NANTUCKET STYLE

2 cups bay scallops, washed,
    drained and dried
flour
1 cup half-and-half

2 tablespoons butter
1 teaspoon salt
½ teaspoon pepper

Preheat oven to 350° F.

Dredge the scallops with flour and put into a greased casserole. Pour on the half-and-half, dot with butter, and season with salt and pepper.

Bake for 30 minutes, and serve from the casserole.

*4 servings*　　　　　　　　　　　　　　　　　　　　　　　*quick*

## OLD-FASHIONED SCALLOP BROIL

1 garlic clove, cut
6 tablespoons butter, melted
1 pound scallops
½ teaspoon salt
½ teaspoon white pepper

few grains of cayenne
flour
1 teaspoon paprika
lemon slices

Rub the bottom and sides of a shallow baking dish or pie pan with the garlic. Add half of the melted butter, and swish around.

Arrange the scallops in the dish. Season with salt, pepper and a little cayenne, and dust lightly with flour and paprika. Pour on the remaining butter.

Slide under the broiler, and cook for 10 minutes, or until golden. Serve with lemon slices.

*4 servings*　　　　　　　　　　　　　　　　　　　　　　　*quick*

## SCALLOPS EN BROCHETTE

1 pound scallops
8 slices of bacon, quartered
1 cup mushroom caps
1 garlic clove, crushed
1 scallion, minced

2 tablespoons chopped
   parsley
2 tablespoons olive oil
2 tablespoons butter

Preheat oven to broil, or 500° F.

Thread the scallops, bacon slices and mushrooms alternately on 4 skewers, and cook under the broiler until brown on all sides.

Meanwhile in a small saucepan gently sauté the garlic, scallion and parsley in the oil and butter, without browning.

Pour the sauce over the skewered scallops.

*4 servings* *quick*

## SKEWERED BAYS

6 slices of bacon
24 bay scallops
1 egg, lightly beaten with 1
   cup milk

flour
24 stuffed olives, warmed

Broil the bacon in a heavy skillet until nearly crisp. Remove, cut slices into quarters, and set aside.

Dip the scallops into the egg-milk mixture, dredge with flour, and fry quickly in the bacon fat.

Remove from the skillet and thread alternately onto small wooden picks or skewers with bacon bits and stuffed olives, one of each per skewer.

*24 skewers* *quick*

## SCALLOPED SCALLOPS

¼ pound butter
1½ cups cracker crumbs
2 eggs, beaten
1 teaspoon salt

½ teaspoon pepper
dash of Tabasco
2 cups bay scallops, or sea
    scallops cut into halves

Melt the butter in a saucepan. Stir in the cracker crumbs, eggs and seasonings, and remove from heat.

Preheat oven to 350° F.

Butter a 2-quart casserole and put in the cracker-crumb mixture and scallops in alternate layers, with crumbs on top.

Bake for 30 minutes. Serve from the casserole.

*4 to 6 servings*                                        *quick*

## SCALLOPS AND MUSHROOMS

1 pound bay scallops or sea
    scallops cut up
1 cup clam broth
½ pound mushrooms,
    cleaned and chopped
4 tablespoons butter

2 tablespoons flour
1 cup milk
1 teaspoon salt
dash of cayenne
1 lemon, cut

Simmer the scallops gently in the clam broth for 3 to 5 minutes; drain, reserving the broth.

Sauté the mushrooms in 2 tablespoons butter for 5 minutes. Stir in the flour and cook for 3 minutes longer. Stir in the milk and seasonings until thickened. Add some of reserved broth if necessary to give sauce correct texture.

Melt the remaining 2 tablespoons butter and stir it and the scallops into the mushroom sauce.

Pile into 4 scallop shells, squeeze a little lemon juice onto each, and serve.

*4 servings*                                        *quick*

# SCALLOPS NEWBURG

1 pound scallops
2 tablespoons butter
½ teaspoon paprika
1 teaspoon salt
½ cup sherry

2 cups half-and-half
2 tablespoons flour
2 egg yolks
8 toast points

Sauté the scallops gently in butter for a few minutes (longer for sea scallops). Add seasonings and sherry.

Mix 1 cup of the half-and-half with the flour until smooth, then add the second cup. Stir into the scallops until mixture thickens.

Remove from heat, stir in the egg yolks, and spoon onto toast points.

*4 servings*                                                        *quick*

---

# SCALLOP SEVICHE

This interesting recipe, from south of the border, "cooks" bits of raw fish by marinating them in citrus juices. Serve as an appetizer with drinks. Or serve scallops raw and unmarinated with a variety of sauces for dipping.

2 pounds raw bay scallops, or
    sea scallops cut into
    halves
1 tablespoon ground red chili
2 onions, thinly sliced

1 garlic clove, finely chopped
¼ teaspoon freshly ground
    pepper
1 cup lime juice
1 cup lemon juice

Mix all the ingredients together and place into a deep glass dish so that the scallops are covered with the marinade.

Cover and refrigerate for 4 hours, or until scallops are well "cooked"; they will become opaque as if poached.

Drain and serve on food picks.

*6 servings*

# *MUSSELS*

Mussels are a delicate bivalve with a thin blue-black shell measuring from 2 to 2½ inches long. Found in all the oceans of the world, the best ones come from colder New England waters. They are also bred commercially in saltwater pools and marketed live in the shell, or canned.

Mussels may be prepared in almost any way that clams and oysters are.

## MUSSELS, NEWPORT STYLE

| | |
|---|---|
| 4 dozen mussels in shells | ½ cup dry white wine |
| 1 teaspoon minced onion | ½ teaspoon salt |
| 3 slices of crisp bacon, crumbled | ½ teaspoon paprika |
| | ½ teaspoon crumbled dill |

Scrub the mussels and soak in a large pot of fresh water for 2 hours. Discard any that float. The fresh water will make the mussels plump.

Pour off the water, leaving only a cup full. Add a little salt, cover the pot, and steam for 3 minutes, or until shells open. Remove mussels from shells; discard shells. Strain the broth and set aside.

Preheat oven to 325° F.

Place the mussels into a casserole, add the onion, bacon crumbles, wine, strained broth and seasonings. Bake for 15 minutes.

Serve from the casserole, with crusty bread to mop up the broth.

*4 servings*

## BAKED MUSSELS WITH BACON

3 dozen mussels, well
   scrubbed
2 teaspoons salt
1 teaspoon pepper

½ cup minced onion
8 strips of bacon
½ cup grated American
   cheese

Preheat oven to 300° F.

Open the mussels as you would clams, and remove the beards. Leave each mussel in the bottom shell, like clams on the half-shell.

Arrange half-shells side by side in a shallow baking pan, and sprinkle with salt, pepper and minced onion.

Lay the bacon strips on top, sprinkle with cheese, and bake until bacon is crisp.

*4 servings*                                                    *quick*

## MUSSELS MARINIÈRE

¼ pound butter
3 tablespoons chopped
   shallots or scallions
pinch of dried thyme
¼ bay leaf
4 dozen fresh mussels, well
   scrubbed and debearded

½ teaspoon salt
½ teaspoon white pepper
1 cup dry white wine
½ cup heavy cream mixed
   with 2 egg yolks
2 teaspoons minced parsley

Melt the butter in a large saucepan and gently sauté the shallots, thyme and bay leaf for a minute or so.

Add the mussels (only those with tightly closed shells), sprinkle with salt and pepper, and pour on the wine. Cover and cook over high heat for 10 minutes, or until shells open.

Remove the mussels, still in shells, to 4 heated soup bowls. Strain the liquid, and thicken with the cream and egg-yolk mixture.

Pour the sauce over the mussels, sprinkle with minced parsley, and serve with crusty French bread.

*4 servings*                                                    *quick*

## FRIED MUSSELS

4 dozen fresh mussels,
   scrubbed and debearded
½ cup olive oil
juice of 1 lemon
2 tablespoons chopped
   parsley

½ teaspoon salt
½ teaspoon white pepper
flour
fat for deep-frying

Place the mussels (only those with tightly closed shells) into a saucepan, cover with water, and cook for 10 minutes, or until shells open.

Remove mussels from the shells and marinate in oil, lemon juice and parsley for 30 minutes.

Drain, season with salt and pepper, dredge with flour, and fry in deep fat.

*4 servings*                                                 *quick*

## OYSTERS

These bivalve mollusks are scavengers. They grow in the shallow waters of bays, sounds and river mouths where there is plenty of food, and where the saltiness of the sea has been diluted by the flow of fresh water from the land.

Most American oysters come from the waters of the Chesapeake Bay and those surrounding Long Island. New England's oysters are taken mostly from the Cape Cod area.

Oysters are nutritious—rich in proteins, minerals and vitamins—and are easy to prepare and easy to serve. They can be eaten raw, broiled, fried, scalloped, baked or stewed.

## CAPE COD OYSTER FRY

| | |
|---|---|
| 1 quart shucked oysters | 1 cup bread crumbs, cracker |
| salt | crumbs or cornmeal |
| pepper | butter |
| 2 eggs, lightly beaten | cooking fat |
| 2 tablespoons milk or cream | |

Drain the oysters, pat them dry with a napkin, and season with salt and pepper.

Mix the eggs and milk or cream. Dip the oysters into this mixture, and roll in crumbs.

Fry in a 50–50 mixture of butter and fat for about 5 minutes, or until golden brown on both sides. Fat must be heated to the smoking point.

*4 to 6 servings*                                                                          *quick*

*"In the long try watches of the night it is a common thing for the seamen to dip their ship-biscuit into the huge oil-pots and let them fry there awhile. Many a good supper have I thus made."* Moby-Dick, *Herman Melville*

## NEWPORT OYSTERS

| | |
|---|---|
| 1 pint shucked oysters | ½ teaspoon pepper |
| 4 tablespoons olive oil | dash of Tabasco |
| 4 tablespoons chopped | ½ teaspoon Worcestershire |
| shallots | sauce |
| 4 tablespoons chopped | 1 cup dry white wine |
| parsley | flour |
| 1 garlic clove, minced | 2 tablespoons butter |
| ½ teaspoon salt | |

Preheat oven to 300° F.

Drain the oysters and reserve the liquor.

Put 2 tablespoons olive oil into a shallow baking dish, add the oysters, and then 2 more tablespoons olive oil. Add the herbs, seasonings, wine, and about half of the oyster liquor.

Sift a little flour over the top, dot with butter, and bake for 15 to 20 minutes, or until brown on top.

Serve with good crusty French bread.

*4 to 6 servings*                                                                              *quick*

## CREAMED OYSTERS, PLYMOUTH STYLE

1 pint shucked oysters
¼ pound butter
½ cup flour
2 cups light cream or milk

1 teaspoon minced fresh dill
salt
white pepper

Simmer the oysters in their liquor for 5 minutes, or until the edges begin to curl. Drain oysters, but reserve ½ cup of the liquor.

Melt butter in the top section of a double boiler, blend in flour, add cream and reserved oyster liquor, and cook until thickened, stirring constantly.

Add oysters and dill, heat, and season to taste. Serve in patty shells or on toast.

*4 to 6 servings*                                                                              *quick*

# *LOBSTER*

Largest of the crustaceans, the lobster is found in the cold waters of the North Atlantic from Labrador to North Carolina, but by far the bulk of the catch is made along the coasts of Maine and Massachusetts. A European species differing somewhat in size, shape and coloration is found in the Northern European waters.

The lobster reaches full growth slowly, more than 6 years being required to produce the minimum legal marketable size. Although creatures have been taken weighing 20 pounds or more, in the market they weigh from 1 to 3 pounds. They are graded as *chickens* (¾ to 1 pound), *quarters* (1¼ pounds), *large* (1½ to 2¼ pounds) and *jumbo* (over 2½ pounds).

Lobsters are sold live, cooked in the shell, or frozen. Lobster meat cooked and removed from the shell is available iced, frozen or canned.

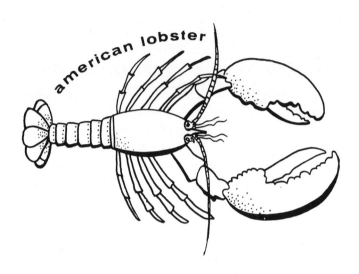

## BOILED LOBSTER

| | |
|---|---|
| 4 live lobsters, 1½ pounds each | 6 tablespoons salt |
| 4 quarts boiling water | melted butter |
| | lemon wedges |

Plunge lobsters head first into boiling salted water * and continue cooking for 20 minutes. Drain.

Place lobsters on their backs and cut lengthwise into halves. Remove the stomach (just back of the head) and the intestinal vein.

Serve hot with melted butter and lemon, or cold with mayonnaise.

*4 servings*                                           *quick*

* Or place them in cold water and bring the water to a boil. Scientific experiments made to ascertain which is the more humane way to kill a lobster revealed the following surprising results: lobsters placed in cold water appeared to expire gradually and painlessly as the temperature of the water increased, while those plunged alive into boiling water made violent attempts to escape, remaining alive up to a full minute. Or simply sever spinal cord before boiling.

## BROILED LOBSTER

4 live lobsters, 1½ pounds
   each
4 tablespoons butter
½ teaspoon salt

½ teaspoon white pepper
½ teaspoon paprika
lemon wedges
melted butter

Kill the lobsters by inserting the point of a knife between the body
and the tail sections. Place lobsters on their backs and cut lengthwise into halves. Remove the stomach (just in back of the head)
and the intestinal vein. Crack the claws.

Place lobsters on a broiler pan, brush with butter, and sprinkle
with salt, pepper and paprika. Broil about 4 inches from the
source of heat for 12 to 15 minutes, or until lightly browned.

Garnish with lemon wedges and serve with melted butter.

*4 servings*                                               *quick*

---

## BAKED STUFFED LOBSTER

4 live lobsters, 1¼ pounds
   each
3 cups soft bread cubes

4 tablespoons butter, melted
2 tablespoons grated onion
1 garlic clove, minced

Cook and clean the lobsters; remove and save the green liver and
coral.

Preheat oven to 400° F.

Mix together the bread cubes, butter, onion, garlic, liver and
coral. Place this stuffing in the body cavities and spread over the
tail meat.

Place in a shallow baking pan or on a baking sheet, and bake for
20 to 25 minutes, or until golden.

*4 servings*                                               *quick*

VARIATION: Add a cup of grated cheese to the stuffing.

## BAR HARBOR LOBSTER PIE

6 tablespoons butter
¼ cup sherry
1 cup lobster meat
2 tablespoons flour
¾ cup light cream mixed
    with 2 egg yolks, lightly
    beaten

¼ cup cracker crumbs mixed
    with ½ teaspoon paprika
2 tablespoons grated cheese

Melt 2 tablespoons butter; stir in the sherry and lobster meat and set aside.

Melt 3 tablespoons butter, stir in the flour, and cook for about 1 minute. Remove from heat and stir in the cream-egg mixture.

Add the wine and lobster meat to the sauce and stir constantly over very low heat until smooth and thick. Do not allow to boil or sauce may curdle.

Preheat oven to 300° F.

Transfer lobster mixture to a deep-dish pie plate. Sprinkle with cracker-crumb mixture, top with grated cheese, and dot with remaining butter. Bake, uncovered, for 10 minutes, or until browned.

*4 servings*

## LOBSTER CROQUETTES

6 tablespoons butter
6 tablespoons flour
1 teaspoon salt
dash of pepper
1 cup milk
1 teaspoon lemon juice
2 cups chopped cooked
    lobster meat

fat for deep-frying
dry bread crumbs
1 egg, lightly beaten with 2
    tablespoons water
dash of cayenne
1 cup half milk, half cream
½ cup chopped green olives

Melt 4 tablespoons butter over very low heat and stir in 4 tablespoons flour, ½ teaspoon salt and dash of pepper until smooth. Gradually add the milk, stirring until mixture thickens.

Add the lemon juice and lobster; mix and chill.

Heat fat to 390° F.

Form lobster mixture into croquettes, roll in bread crumbs, then in the egg mixture, then in bread crumbs again.

Put the croquettes a few at a time into a frying basket and fry until golden brown.

Meanwhile, melt remaining 2 tablespoons butter over very low heat, stir in 2 tablespoons flour, ½ teaspoon salt and the cayenne, then the half-and-half. Continue stirring until mixture is smooth and thickened. Stir in the chopped olives and pour over the croquettes.

*4 servings*

blue crab

## CRABS

The crab is one of the most interesting of all shellfish. It ranges in size all the way from the giant Alaska King crab weighing 8 to 10 pounds and the Pacific Dungeness sometimes measuring a foot across to the tiny oyster crab.

The most plentiful and perhaps most prized of all crabs is the blue crab, found along the Atlantic Coast from Cape Cod to Florida. This scrappy creature measures up to 6 inches across, is dark green on top and creamy white beneath, and has large bluish claws.

Crabs are available in the market live or cooked. The meat comes pasteurized, frozen and canned.

## CRABMEAT CASSEROLE WITH CHEESE

6 tablespoons butter
4 tablespoons flour
¼ cup water
1 cup half-and-half
½ pound freshly cooked
    backfin crabmeat from
    blue crabs

¼ cup chopped green pepper
1 pimiento, chopped
2 hard-cooked eggs, chopped
1 teaspoon salt
½ cup bread crumbs
½ cup grated Cheddar cheese

Preheat oven to 350° F.

Melt 4 tablespoons butter, blend in the flour, stir in the water, then the half-and-half. Simmer, stirring, until smooth and thickened.

Add the crab, green pepper, pimiento, eggs and salt. Stir carefully, to avoid breaking up the crab lumps.

Transfer to a buttered 1-quart casserole. Top with bread crumbs, dot with remaining butter, and sprinkle with cheese. Bake for 30 minutes, or until golden.

*4 servings*

## CRAB CAKES

1 pound freshly cooked
    crabmeat from blue crabs
½ teaspoon dry mustard
2 tablespoons mayonnaise
1 egg, beaten
½ teaspoon salt

dash of cayenne
2 slices of bread, wet and
    squeezed out
4 tablespoons bread crumbs
    or cornmeal
fat for frying

Combine the crabmeat with the mustard, mayonnaise, egg, salt, cayenne and moistened bread. Shape into 4 cakes and roll in bread crumbs or cornmeal.

Heat fat in a heavy frying pan. Add the cakes and cook at moderate heat until brown on one side, then turn and brown on the other. Or fry the cakes in deep fat.

*4 servings*                                                              *quick*

## DEVILED CRABS

1 pound freshly cooked
    crabmeat from blue crabs
¼ teaspoon dry mustard
¼ teaspoon grated mace
dash of cayenne
1 tablespoon chopped parsley

1 teaspoon Worcestershire
    sauce
3 tablespoons melted butter
1 tablespoon lemon juice
1 egg, beaten
¼ cup dry bread crumbs

Preheat oven to 350° F.

Add the seasonings to the crabmeat. Stir in the melted butter, lemon juice and beaten egg.

Divide among 4 well-buttered shells or ramekins, and sprinkle with bread crumbs. Bake in oven for 15 minutes, or until golden.

*4 servings*                                                         *quick*

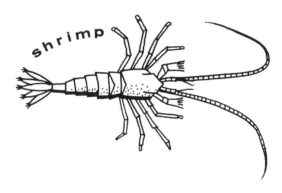

## SHRIMPS

Live shrimps are pale green-gray in color and semitransparent, but turn pink upon cooking.

Shrimps are marketed all over the country—fresh, frozen, frozen-peeled and canned—in sizes ranging from 16 to a pound to 10. Giant deepwater shrimps have been taken in the Gulf of Mexico weighing as much as ¼ pound each.

Only the tail meat of the shrimp is eaten, the head and thorax having been removed before marketing.

## SHRIMP CASSEROLE

1½ cups cooked peeled
   shrimps
2 cups cooked noodles
3 hard-cooked eggs,
   quartered
1 onion, thinly sliced
1 cup sliced mushrooms
2 tablespoons butter

2 tablespoons flour
1 teaspoon salt
½ teaspoon pepper
½ teaspoon celery salt
1½ cups milk
bread crumbs
butter

Preheat oven to 375° F.

Put the shrimps, noodles, eggs, onion and mushrooms into a 2-quart casserole.

Melt the butter; sitr in the flour and seasonings, then the milk. Cook, stirring, until sauce is smooth and thickened. Add sauce to the casserole.

Sprinkle with bread crumbs, dot with butter, and bake for about 20 minutes, or until crumbs are brown. Serve from the casserole.

*4 to 6 servings*

## BEER-FRIED SHRIMPS

1½ pounds peeled raw
   shrimps
½ teaspoon Worcestershire
   sauce
½ cup flour
pinch of salt
1 teaspoon melted butter

1 egg, beaten
½ cup beer
fat for deep-frying
2 tablespoons minced
   cranberries mixed with 2
   tablespoons fresh
   horseradish

Brush the shrimps well with Worcestershire.

Sift the flour and salt together; stir in the butter, egg and beer until mixture is smooth.

Heat fat to 365° F.

Dip the shrimps, a few at a time, into the batter. Fry in deep fat for 3 to 5 minutes, or until golden. Serve with horseradish-cranberry sauce.

*4 servings*                                                                 *quick*

## BAKED STUFFED SHRIMPS

8 large shrimps, peeled and
    cooked
2 cups soft bread crumbs
4 tablespoons melted butter
2 tablespoons mayonnaise
1 teaspoon dry mustard

2 tablespoons minced onion
1 garlic clove, minced
1 teaspoon salt
½ teaspoon pepper
few grains of cayenne

Preheat oven to 400° F.

Split the shrimps nearly through and open up butterfly style.

Mix together the remaining ingredients and pile onto the shrimps. Place on a shallow baking pan and bake for 20 minutes, or until golden.

*4 servings*                                                          *quick*

## SAUTÉED SHRIMPS, MUSTARD SAUCE

2 pounds peeled fresh shrimps
1 teaspoon salt
2 tablespoons butter
2 tablespoons dry mustard
1 teaspoon flour

¼ teaspoon salt
1 teaspoon sugar
½ cup heavy cream
1 egg yolk
½ cup warm vinegar

Salt the shrimps and sauté in butter for 5 minutes on each side. Skewer with food picks and keep warm.

Put into the top part of a double boiler the mustard, flour, salt, sugar and cream. Heat, stirring, for 5 minutes. Beat in the egg yolk and then the vinegar. Serve as a dip for the shrimps.

*4 to 6 servings*                                                     *quick*

## MIXED SEAFOOD CASSEROLE, NANTUCKET

1 cup raw bay scallops
1 cup shelled raw shrimps
1 cup flaked cooked flounder
1 cup chopped mushrooms
1 medium-size onion, chopped
1 cup clam broth

6 tablespoons butter
1 teaspoon salt
½ teaspoon pepper
4 tablespoons flour
2 cups milk
¼ cup sherry

Cook together in a 2-quart casserole the scallops, shrimps, flaked fish, mushrooms, onion, clam broth, 2 tablespoons of the butter, salt and pepper for 3 minutes. Remove from the heat and set aside.

Preheat oven to 300° F.

In a heavy skillet melt remaining butter, stir in the flour, and blend in the milk until sauce is smooth and thickened.

Stir the sauce into the casserole, add the sherry, and bake in the oven for 15 minutes. Serve from the casserole.

*8 servings*                                                                        *quick*

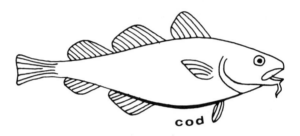

cod

## COD

Cod is probably the most prolific of New England food fishes. In Colonial days it was a culinary mainstay, served fresh in summer and fall and salted or smoked the rest of the year. During the Revolutionary War it remained supreme, and in 1784 a five-foot model was hung in the Massachusetts government house as a memorial to the importance of cod fishery to the Commonwealth. Today the "Sacred Cod" still hangs in the State House in Boston.

As a food fish the cod is one of the most available and versatile of all fish. There's smoked cod, salt cod, fresh cod, whole cod, codfish steaks, flaked cod; there's codfish cheeks and tongue, codfish roe, cod liver . . .

---

*"John Gardner, a mariner of Salem, a half share on condition that he come to Nantucket 'to inhabit and to sett up the trade of ffishing with a sufficient vessel fitt for the taking of Codd ffish.' "* Quaint Nantucket, *William Root Bliss*

---

## COD STEAKS WITH EGG SAUCE

6 codfish steaks, ¾ inch thick
⅜ pound butter
3 hard-cooked eggs, chopped

3 tablespoons minced parsley
salt and pepper

Place the cod slices into a large skillet or poacher, cover with salted water, and simmer for 5 to 8 minutes, or until fish just flakes when fork-tested. Transfer with a slotted spatula to a heated platter. Reserve ½ cup of the poaching liquid.

In a saucepan melt the butter; stir in ½ cup of the poaching liquid, the eggs and the parsley. Season to taste. Boil up for a minute or so and pour the sauce over the fish.

*6 servings*                                                        *quick*

## PORTUGUESE CODFISH

6 medium-size potatoes
2 pounds fresh codfish fillets
4 tablespoons olive oil
2 onions, sliced
5 tablespoons butter
4 tablespoons flour

1¼ cups milk
1½ cups chicken broth
2 tablespoons tomato paste
¼ teaspoon salt
6 hard-cooked eggs, sliced

Put potatoes on to boil in water to cover. Cut codfish into bite-size pieces.

Heat olive oil in a large skillet and sauté onions until lightly browned. Add the codfish. Continue to simmer.

Melt 4 tablespoons butter, stir in flour, and add 1 cup milk gradually while stirring. Add chicken broth. When thick, add tomato paste, cover, and set aside.

Peel 2 potatoes and mash with ¼ cup milk, 1 tablespoon butter and the salt. Slice the rest.

Preheat oven to 350° F.

Starting with codfish and onions, put half in a 2-quart baking dish, then add half of the sliced potatoes, sliced eggs and sauce. Repeat. Spread mashed potatoes on top.

Bake for 35 to 45 minutes, until mashed potatoes are brown.

*6 servings*

## YANKEE CODFISH WITH GRAVY

| | |
|---|---|
| 2 pounds salt codfish | 1 teaspoon salt |
| 3 tablespoons butter | 1½ cups milk |
| 3 tablespoons flour | 2 hard-cooked eggs, chopped |

Cover the codfish with cold water and slowly bring almost to the simmering point. Do not boil or the fish will become tough. Drain and repeat several times until salt has been washed away. Transfer to a heated platter and keep warm.

In a saucepan melt the butter over very low heat; stir in the flour and salt. Gradually add the milk, blending well until sauce has thickened. Stir in the hard-cooked eggs.

Pour the sauce over the fish and serve with hot baked potatoes and Harvard beets.

*4 servings*                                                                                  *quick*

---

## PORTUGUESE SALT COD

| | |
|---|---|
| 2 pounds salt cod | 1 green pepper, sliced |
| 5 medium-size potatoes, peeled and sliced | ¼ cup olive oil |
| 4 medium-size onions, sliced | ¼ teaspoon freshly ground pepper |
| 3 tomatoes, sliced | ¼ teaspoon dried orégano |

Preheat oven to 325° F.

Soak fish in cold water overnight. Remove skin and bones and cut fish into large serving pieces.

In a 2½-quart casserole put a layer of potatoes, then fish, then one of onions, tomatoes and green pepper. Repeat until all is used.

Mix olive oil, pepper and orégano, and pour slowly over all the casserole. Bake for 1½ hours.

This dish can be simmered in a Dutch oven on top of the stove for the same length of time if preferred.

*6 servings*                                                                          *make ahead*

## BAKED COD WITH CLAM STUFFING

1 medium-size onion, minced
4 tablespoons butter
pinch each of thyme, basil,
    paprika and pepper
2 cups fresh bread crumbs
1 egg, beaten
1 cup chopped clams, with
    juice
1 cod, about 4 pounds,
    dressed

1 teaspoon salt
¼ teaspoon pepper
2 tablespoons melted butter
    mixed with dash of
    Tabasco
3 strips of bacon
1 lemon, sliced

Mix together the first 6 ingredients to make the stuffing, reserving a few bread crumbs for later use.

Preheat oven to 400° F.

Wipe the fish dry, and season inside and out with salt and pepper. Stuff loosely with the clam and bread-crumb mixture, and brush with the Tabasco butter.

Place stuffed fish in a greased baking pan. Cover with reserved bread crumbs and bacon strips. Bake for 30 to 40 minutes, 10 minutes per pound.

Serve garnished with lemon slices.

*6 servings*

## CODFISH BALLS OR CAKES

Wouldn't New Englanders be surprised to learn that codfish balls are a popular dish served frequently in the restaurants of Portugal? True, and what's more, it might even be possible that codfish balls were introduced to the New England seaports by fishermen from Portugal.

4 medium-size potatoes,
    peeled and quartered
1 cup salt cod, rinsed and
    shredded

1 egg, beaten
1 tablespoon butter
⅛ teaspoon pepper
fat for deep-frying

Cover potatoes and codfish with water, bring to a boil, and simmer until potatoes are soft.

Drain, return to the stove, and shake until moisture is evaporated. Mash thoroughly.

Add egg, butter and pepper, and form into balls or cakes. Fry in deep fat heated to 390° F. until golden, or sauté in butter.

*4 servings*

## COD TONGUES AND CHEEKS

1 pound fresh cod tongues          2 tablespoons butter
   and cheeks                         parsley
salt and pepper                    lemon wedges
yellow cornmeal, or flour

Pat dry the tongues and cheeks. Season lightly with salt and pepper, and roll in cornmeal or flour. Sauté in butter until golden.

Serve garnished with parsley and lemon wedges.

*4 servings*                                              *quick*

## COD TONGUES AND CHEEKS ON STICKS

Sauté fresh tongues and cheeks in hot olive oil with a garlic clove for 2 minutes.

Add 1 teaspoon vinegar, and a pinch each of thyme, bay leaf and cayenne, and sauté for 10 minutes longer.

Remove from the heat, sprinkle with chopped fennel, and leave to cool in their own juices.

Serve cold on food picks.

*quick*

## SAUTÉED CODFISH ROE

1 large codfish roe
flour
salt and pepper

2 tablespoons butter
4 slices of bacon, cooked
4 lemon wedges

Tie the roe in cheesecloth, place in a skillet, and cover with salted water. Poach gently for 30 minutes. Drain roe and chill in the refrigerator for 12 hours.

Carefully remove cheesecloth and cut roe into ½-inch slices. Sprinkle the slices lightly with flour, season, and sauté in hot butter until golden.

Serve garnished with bacon and lemon slices.

*4 servings*

---

## PANBROILED SCROD

The young cod, known as scrod, more delicate in texture and sweeter in flavor, weighing about 2 pounds, is a favorite New England delicacy in the spring.

2 scrod, 2 pounds each,
    dressed and split
2 tablespoons olive oil mixed
    with 2 tablespoons
    melted butter

1 teaspoon salt
½ teaspoon pepper
flour
minced parsley
lemon slices

Brush the scrod with the oil-butter mixture, season with salt and pepper, and dust lightly with flour.

Heat an oiled heavy skillet and panbroil the scrod for 3 to 5 minutes on each side, or until golden. Sprinkle with minced parsley and serve garnished with lemon slices.

*4 servings*                                          *quick*

# HERRING

When spring comes and ordinary people are hailing the first robin, Nantucketers and Cape Codders are getting all worked up over the annual herring runs.

Each year at the time of the vernal equinox the herring leave the waters of the ocean and swim up the streams to the pond or lake where they were born. Their purpose: to spawn and produce a new generation.

The herring of Nantucket and Cape Cod run about 6 inches in length and are known as "alewives." So prolific are they and so picturesque is the run that people drive for miles to witness the spectacle. The little fish caught up in their own traffic jam are easy prey to "fishermen" who easily dip them out of stream or pond with net or basket—or even catch them by bare hands. Many people keep only the roe-swollen females, tossing the males back into the water.

The roe, smaller than shad roe, is very much prized. Alewives themselves have a delicious, sweet flavor but, like their cousins the shad, they are cursed with a multitude of hairlike bones. Alewives can be filleted: place on a board and loosen and peel off the skin with a sharp paring knife, starting with the tail. Split the fish into halves just above the center bone, turn, and cut away the other half. Discard the bones.

Alewives are preserved by smoking or salting, or they are served fresh by broiling, baking or sautéing.

## BEER-BAKED ALEWIVES

12 fresh alewives, dressed,
   with heads and tails
   removed
ground allspice and cloves

salt and pepper
1 onion, thinly sliced
¾ cup beer
¼ cup vinegar

Preheat oven to 450° F.

Sprinkle the alewives with the seasonings and place them in a shallow baking dish. Arrange onion slices over them.

Mix together the beer and vinegar, pour over the fish, cover, and bake for 25 minutes.

*4 to 6 servings*                                        *quick*

## SAUTÉED ALEWIVES

12 fresh alewives, dressed,
   with heads and tails
   removed
salt and pepper
flour

1 medium-size onion,
   chopped
1 tablespoon butter
juice of 1 lemon

Wash and dry the fish, sprinkle with salt and pepper, and dredge with flour.

Sauté the onion in butter in a heavy skillet until golden. Add the alewives and sauté for 10 minutes, turning once. Transfer to a heated platter.

Stir the lemon juice into the pan and pour over the fish.

*4 to 6 servings*                                        *quick*

## PICKLED HERRING

8 herring fillets, cut into
   serving pieces
1 onion, sliced
1 garlic clove, crushed
2 bay leaves

1 tablespoon whole allspice
   berries
1 cup white vinegar
1 cup water

Soak the herring pieces in brine strong enough to float a potato for 24 hours or longer.

Remove from brine, rinse, and add the remaining ingredients.

Store in a cool place until ready for use. Or drain and pack in jars with sour cream.

## SPICED MACKEREL

½ cup salt
1 tablespoon each of ground
  cinnamon, allspice and
  cloves

12 small mackerel, dressed
1 quart vinegar

Preheat oven to 250° F.

Mix salt and spices. Roll the mackerel in the mixture, and lay them in an ovenproof jar. Cover with vinegar. Bake for 6 hours.

Store in refrigerator.

## BAKED WHOLE HADDOCK

The following recipe will serve for baking almost any large whole fish. If desired, the cavity of the fish may be loosely stuffed with bread stuffing or your favorite variation: celery stuffing, herb stuffing, mushroom stuffing, crabmeat stuffing or shrimp stuffing.

1 whole haddock, dressed
salt

lemon slices
minced parsley

Preheat oven to 375° F.

Cut a few gashes across sides of fish, rub inside and out with salt, and place on a greased rack in an uncovered shallow pan.

Bake, allowing 10 minutes per pound for fish under 4 pounds and 15 minutes per pound for larger fish. If fish seems dry, lay strips of bacon over top of fish.

Serve garnished with lemon slices and minced parsley.

*quick*

## BAKED HADDOCK WITH CHEESE

1 cup milk
½ cup flour
1 tablespoon dry mustard
1 cup grated American
    cheese

1 teaspoon salt
2 pounds haddock fillets
butter

Preheat oven to 350° F.

Mix together into a thick sauce the milk, flour, mustard, cheese and salt, using a wire whisk.

Place layers of fillets and sauce in a buttered casserole and bake for about 1 hour.

*4 servings*                                          *quick*

---

## HADDOCK CASSEROLE

4 pounds haddock, dressed
2 cups milk
¼ onion
1 parsley sprig
½ cup flour
2 egg yolks, slightly beaten

½ teaspoon pepper
¼ teaspoon dried thyme
1 teaspoon salt
4 tablespoons butter
½ cup cracker crumbs
½ cup grated cheese

Boil the haddock for 10 minutes. Drain, discard the bones and skin, and flake the flesh with a fork.

In a saucepan simmer 1 cup of the milk, the onion and parsley.

Stir the flour into the remaining cup of milk until smooth and add to saucepan. Stir until thickened. Stir in the egg yolks, seasonings and butter.

Preheat oven to 350° F.

Butter a 2-quart casserole and put in the flaked fish and sauce in alternate layers, with the sauce on top.

Sprinkle cracker crumbs and cheese on top. Bake for 30 minutes.

*6 servings*                                          *quick*

## FINNAN HADDIE IN MILK

The firm, white, flavorful meat of the haddock is much improved, say many seafood lovers, by salting and smoking over a smoldering oak fire. The smoked product will keep for a long time without refrigeration.

Some of the salt is usually removed by soaking or simmering, but care should be exercised not to overdo or the rich smoky flavor might be lost.

| | |
|---|---|
| 2 pounds finnan haddie | 2 tablespoons butter |
| 1 cup milk | pepper |

Cover the fish with water and simmer for a few minutes. Drain.

Add the milk and butter and cook, covered, over moderate heat for 15 minutes.

Sprinkle with pepper and serve.

*6 servings*                                                          *quick*

## FINNAN HADDIE, NANTUCKET STYLE

| | |
|---|---|
| 2 pounds finnan haddie | 2 tablespoons flour |
| 1 cup milk | 1 cup cubed cooked potatoes |
| ⅛ pound salt pork, cubed | 2 eggs, slightly beaten |

Cover finnan haddie with water and simmer for a few minutes. Drain.

Cook finnan haddie in milk for 15 minutes. Drain, reserve the milk, and separate fish into flakes with a fork.

Cook the salt pork in a heavy skillet until brown and crisp. Remove and reserve the scraps, leaving fat in the skillet.

Stir the flour into fat until well blended. Stir in the reserved milk, adding more milk if necessary.

Add the potatoes and cook, stirring, until browned. Add the pork scraps and flaked fish. Stir in the eggs and serve.

*4 servings*                                                          *quick*

# SCUP COATUE

4 scup, filleted
milk
¼ cup cornmeal
1 teaspoon salt

½ teaspoon pepper
butter
lemon slices

Dip the scup fillets into milk, then roll in cornmeal. Season with salt and pepper.

Fry in butter in a heavy skillet, until crisp and brown. Reduce the heat, cover, and cook slowly for 20 minutes.

Serve with lemon slices.

*4 servings*                                                                *quick*

---

# BROILED STRIPED BASS, MAÎTRE D'HÔTEL

1 striped bass, 4 to 5 pounds,
    dressed and split
olive oil
1 teaspoon salt
¼ teaspoon pepper
flour

melted butter
Maître d'Hôtel Butter (recipe
    follows)
chopped fresh tarragon
lemon wedges

Preheat broiler to 500° F.

Brush the fish with olive oil, season with salt and pepper, and dust very lightly with flour. Place on a greased broiler rack, skin side down, and slide under the broiler.

Cook for 6 minutes, or until slightly browned. Baste with melted butter, turn, and repeat.

Remove to a heated platter, spread with maître d'hôtel butter, and garnish with chopped tarragon and lemon wedges.

*4 to 6 servings*                                                          *quick*

MAÎTRE D'HÔTEL BUTTER: Mix together over low heat ½ cup melted butter, 2 tablespoons chopped parsley, 1 teaspoon chopped fresh tarragon, ½ teaspoon salt and a little pepper. Beat in, drop by drop, 1 tablespoon lemon juice.

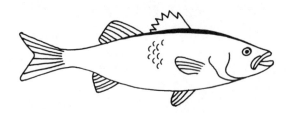

## PANBROILED STRIPED BASS FILLETS

This is a quick, delicious and foolproof method of cooking almost any kind of fish fillets.

| | |
|---|---|
| 1 striped bass fillet, 3 pounds | 1 teaspoon salt |
| flour | ⅛ teaspoon pepper |
| 2 tablespoons butter | paprika |
| 1 teaspoon lemon juice | |

Pat fish dry and flour lightly.

Melt the butter in a heavy skillet, add the lemon juice, and bring to high heat.

Lay the fillet in the pan, brown for a few minutes, and turn. Sprinkle with salt and pepper. Cover, reduce the heat, and cook for about 10 minutes, or until fish flakes when fork-tested.

Serve sprinkled with paprika.

*4 servings*                                                    *quick*

---

## BROILED SEA BASS WITH OLIVE SAUCE

| | |
|---|---|
| 3 pounds black sea bass steak, | ¼ cup sliced olives (ripe, |
| or steaks | green, or stuffed) |
| 1 teaspoon salt | 1 teaspoon paprika |
| 2 tablespoons olive oil | ½ teaspoon pepper |
| 4 tablespoons butter | 2 teaspoons lemon juice. |
| 1 garlic clove, crushed | chopped fresh dill |

Salt the fish steak and panbroil it in a heavy skillet, using as little oil as necessary to prevent sticking. Test with a fork and remove when fish is flaky—3 minutes on each side should do it. Set aside on a warm platter.

Using the same skillet, melt the butter, add the garlic, olives, paprika, pepper and lemon juice, and sauté gently for a few minutes.

Pour the sauce over the steak and garnish with chopped fresh dill.

*4 to 6 servings*                                                    *quick*

---

## BLUEFISH WITH SOUR CREAM

1 bluefish, 6 to 8 pounds, dressed, head and tail removed and split, or 2 smaller fish
1½ cups sour cream

½ cup mayonnaise
2 tablespoons chopped chives
2 tablespoons lemon juice
½ teaspoon salt
¼ teaspoon pepper

Preheat oven to 375° F.

Place fish skin side down in a buttered baking dish.

Mix together the remaining ingredients, spread over the fish, and bake for 30 minutes.

*4 to 6 servings*                                                    *quick*

---

## BLUEFISH WITH CAPER STUFFING

1 bluefish, 8 pounds, dressed, head and tail removed
1 medium-size onion, minced
4 tablespoons butter, softened
1 teaspoon salt
dash of pepper

pinch each of thyme and rosemary
2 cups fresh bread crumbs
2 tablespoons chopped capers
1 small sour pickle, chopped
milk or fish stock

Preheat oven to 375° F.

Mix together all the ingredients except the fish. Moisten with milk or fish stock, and stuff lightly into the cavity of bluefish.

Bake for 1 hour, or until done to your taste.

*6 to 8 servings*                                                    *quick*

## BLUEFISH WITH GIN

This recipe comes by word of mouth from a long list of distinguished Nantucketers, one a descendant of the founding gentry.

| | |
|---|---|
| 1 bluefish fillet, 3 pounds | ¼ teaspoon pepper |
| ¼ cup melted butter | ½ teaspoon salt |
| 3 tablespoons onion flakes | 3 ounces gin |

Preheat broiler to 500° F.

Put fillet in broiler pan or on a sheet of heavy aluminum foil. Pour half of butter over the fish; sprinkle with onion flakes, pepper and salt.

Broil fish 3 inches from the source of heat. When fish starts to brown, mix gin and remaining melted butter and pour over fish. Ignite gin with a match and quickly return to the broiler. Broil fish for 3 to 5 minutes, and turn off heat. Fish will sputter and flame; when the flame dies, the fish is ready.

*4 servings*                                                                    *quick*

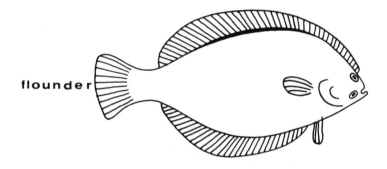

flounder

## *FLOUNDER*

Flounder is the family name for lemon sole, gray sole, dab, fluke, yellowtail and a large number of other flatfish. True sole—Dover sole—are found only in European waters.

The waters of New England abound with flounder in one form or another all summer long.

The flesh of flounders is firm, white, sweet and without oiliness, and the scales are minute. All are eminently suitable for broiling, poaching and frying.

## BROILED WHOLE FLOUNDER

| | |
|---|---|
| 4 small whole flounders, dressed, washed and dried | flour |
| | salt and pepper |
| | paprika |
| 4 tablespoons melted butter | lemon wedges |

Preheat oven broiler to 500° F.

Brush the fish on both sides with butter, dust lightly with flour, and season with salt, pepper and paprika.

Place on a preheated greased broiling rack 3 inches from the source of heat. Broil until golden; turn and repeat.

Serve with lemon wedges.

*4 servings*                                                      *quick*

## FRIED FLOUNDER FILLETS

| | |
|---|---|
| 4 thin slices of ham with fat | flour |
| 4 flounder fillets, about 2 pounds | 2 eggs, beaten |
| | ¼ cup milk |
| ½ teaspoon salt | bread crumbs |

Panbroil the ham in a heavy skillet and remove to a heated platter. Leave ham fat in skillet.

Sprinkle the fillets with salt, roll up, and fasten with wooden picks. Dredge with flour, dip into eggs and then into milk. Fry the fillets in the ham fat, turning to brown all sides.

Place 1 rolled fillet on each of the ham slices and serve.

*4 servings*                                                      *quick*

*"To 'sliver' is to cut each side of a fish away in one piece from the head to the tail, which is the only proper way to clean either of the fish mentioned—flounder, plaice fish, or scup."* from an old Nantucket book

## BAKED STUFFED FLOUNDER

½ cup dry bread crumbs
¼ cup melted butter
8 spring onions, minced
2 tablespoons minced
    watercress

1 cup chopped fresh or
    canned mushrooms
2 hard-cooked eggs, chopped
6 flounder fillets
lemon slices

Preheat oven to 375° F.

Mix together the bread crumbs, butter, onions, watercress, mushrooms and eggs, and spoon some onto each fillet. Roll up the fillets and fasten with wooden picks.

Place in a shallow baking dish and bake for 30 minutes. Serve with lemon slices.

*6 servings* *quick*

---

## CAPE COD FILLETS WITH OYSTERS

2 pounds flounder fillets
¼ pound butter
1 teaspoon lemon juice
1 teaspoon salt

1 dozen medium oysters
1 teaspoon Worcestershire
    sauce
½ cup dry bread crumbs

Panbroil the fillets in butter and lemon juice for about 3 minutes on each side, just until they flake when tested with a fork. Transfer to an oven dish, and season with salt.

Poach the oysters in their own liquid with Worcestershire until edges curl.

Transfer oysters to the oven dish with the fillets, cover all with bread crumbs, and moisten with the oyster liquid. Glaze under the broiler.

*4 servings* *quick*

# POACHED FLOUNDER FILLETS

Fillets can be poached in almost any liquid—milk, cream, white wine, fish stock, clam broth, salted water or a specially prepared *court bouillon*. When the fish has been cooked the liquid may then be used as the basis for a sauce.

2 cups water
2 cups dry white wine
1 onion, thinly sliced
½ bay leaf
pinch of dried thyme
½ teaspoon salt
few peppercorns
4 flounder fillets, about
    2½ pounds total

3 tablespoons butter
2 tablespoons flour
1 teaspoon salt
½ teaspoon pepper
¼ cup milk
1 cup chopped mushrooms
minced parsley

Put first 7 ingredients in a heavy skillet and simmer for 30 minutes.

Put the fillets into this *court bouillon* and cook gently until the flesh flakes when tested with a fork. Remove fish carefully to a heated platter. Strain the *court bouillon* and reserve.

In a separate pan melt the butter, stir in the flour and seasonings, and then the milk until sauce is smooth and thickened.

Add this sauce to the *court bouillon*. Add mushrooms also, then stir and heat. Pour sauce over the fillets, and garnish with parsley.

*4 servings*                                                                 *quick*

# FILLETS OF FLOUNDER AU GRATIN

2 tablespoons chopped
  parsley
2 tablespoons chopped chives
1 cup chopped peeled
  mushrooms
2 pounds flounder fillets
1 teaspoon salt

½ teaspoon white pepper
4 tablespoons butter
1 cup dry white wine or
  water
1 cup fresh bread crumbs
1 cup grated cheese

Preheat oven to 325° F.

Butter a casserole and cover bottom with 1 tablespoon parsley, 1 tablespoon chives and ½ cup mushrooms.

Place fish on top, cover with the remaining parsley, chives and mushrooms, and sprinkle with seasonings. Dot with butter, add the wine, and sprinkle with bread crumbs and cheese.

Bake, uncovered, for 30 minutes. Serve from the casserole.

*4 to 6 servings*                                                    *quick*

# POULTRY &
# GAME BIRDS

## BRAISED CHICKEN

4 thick slices of salt pork, diced
1 frying chicken, cut up
1 garlic clove, peeled
8 small onions, peeled

4 small carrots, cut into 1-inch pieces
1 cup white wine or water
½ teaspoon salt
¼ teaspoon pepper

Preheat oven to 325° F.

Fry out salt pork in a heavy pan until brown. Remove cracklings from pan and reserve. Leave fat in pan.

Halve chicken breasts, separate legs from second joints. Brown chicken pieces on both sides. Add garlic, onions and carrots; brown slightly.

Add wine, salt and pepper, and salt-pork cracklings. Cover and cook in oven for 40 minutes to 1 hour, depending on size of chicken.

*4 to 6 servings*

## OVEN-FRIED CHICKEN

1 frying chicken
½ cup bacon fat

1 cup bread or cracker crumbs

Preheat oven to 325° F.

Disjoint chicken legs and second joints. Separate wings from breast, leaving a good piece of breast on wings to make even servings of dark and white meat.

Dip each piece into bacon fat until well covered and then into bread crumbs. Put in a baking pan. Repeat with all pieces.

Bake for 1 hour, until brown and crisp.

*4 servings*

## CHICKEN BREASTS WITH HAM AND MUSHROOMS

4 tablespoons butter
2 tablespoons olive oil
4 whole chicken breasts, split and boned
4 tablespoons flour
1 small garlic clove, chopped
8 slices of ham

24 large mushrooms
8 pieces of hot buttered toast, crusts removed
½ cup wine
2 tablespoons chopped parsley

Over medium heat melt 2 tablespoons of the butter and the oil in a frying pan large enough to hold the breasts.

Dust the breast pieces with flour and brown for about 8 minutes on each side. Turn heat very low and add garlic to pan juices between slices.

Sauté ham slices in another frying pan for about 1 minute on each side. Put 1 ham slice on each piece of chicken.

Melt remaining 2 tablespoons butter in pan ham was cooked in and sauté mushrooms in it for 3 minutes. Turn, and cook for another 3 minutes.

Put 1 split chicken breast and ham slice on each piece of toast and 3 mushrooms on top. Deglaze pan with wine, and spoon a little over each serving. Serve hot, sprinkled with parsley.

*4 large or 8 small servings*                                    *quick*

## OLD-FASHIONED BARBECUED CHICKEN

This is a popular cookout dish throughout New England; it is usually served with corn cooked in the husk. The recipe that follows serves 4. Double or quadruple it to serve groups of 8 or 16.

2 broiling chickens
½ pound butter
⅓ cup cider vinegar
1 teaspoon dry mustard
1 onion, chopped

1 teaspoon Worcestershire
   sauce
1 teaspoon salt
¼ teaspoon pepper

Prepare a charcoal fire and burn down to white coals.

Split chickens into halves. Remove breast bones. Flatten pieces as much as possible.

Melt butter, add vinegar, mustard, onion, Worcestershire, salt and pepper. Mix well.

Using a pastry brush, brush chicken with sauce and put on grill 5 inches above the coals. Broil for 15 minutes. Turn, brush again, and broil for 15 minutes longer. Repeat this process.

*4 servings*

## PORTUGUESE BARBECUED CHICKEN

2 broiling chickens or fryers
¾ cup olive oil
1 garlic clove, finely chopped

½ teaspoon salt
½ teaspoon pepper

Cut each chicken into halves and then into halves again, leaving a good piece of white meat on each wing piece, and separating legs and second joints.

Mix oil, garlic, salt and pepper. Turn chicken pieces in this mixture. Cover with aluminum foil and refrigerate until ready to use.

Cook on a grill 5 inches above a charcoal fire that has burned down to white coals. Turn often until done, about 20 minutes on each side. Baste with the oil marinade while cooking. Or broil in an oven 5 inches below the source of heat for 20 to 30 minutes on each side.

*8 servings*

# CHICKEN DEVENS

This recipe was given us by a well-known cook who has guests drop in often. She is always ready for them with this very good quick dish.

8 whole chicken breasts
1 package (6 ounces)
    processed wild rice, with
    spices
1 can (10½ ounces)
    condensed cream of
    mushroom soup

2 large cans (8 ounces each)
    mushrooms
1 cup dry sherry
¾ cup sour cream

Preheat oven to 425° F.

In a large frying pan simmer chicken breasts in water barely to cover, about 4 cups, until tender, about 10 minutes. Dice chicken; reserve broth.

Measure 2½ cups broth into saucepan, and add rice and spices; or follow directions on package. Cover tightly and cook over low heat for 20 to 25 minutes.

Combine chicken, rice, soup, mushrooms and sherry, in a buttered 2-quart casserole dish. Bake for 20 minutes. Stir in sour cream, and return to oven for 5 minutes, or until heated through.

*8 to 10 servings*

## CHICKEN AND SCALLOPS

2 large chicken breasts
1 teaspoon salt
¼ teaspoon pepper
2 tablespoons butter
3 tablespoons flour

1 cup broth from cooking
   chicken bones
1 cup light cream
1 pint scallops

Remove bones and skin from breasts, cover with water, and simmer to make 1 cup broth. Add salt and pepper to broth.

Cut chicken breasts into bite-size pieces and sauté pieces in butter over low heat for 5 minutes.

Sprinkle with flour. Add strained broth gradually, stirring all the while. Add cream, then add scallops, and cook without boiling for 5 minutes.

Serve on hot buttered toast or biscuits.

*4 to 6 servings*                                                   *quick*

---

## CHICKEN RISSOLES

1½ cups diced cooked
   chicken
4 tablespoons chicken fat
2 tablespoons parsley flakes,
   or minced fresh parsley
½ teaspoon dried marjoram,
   or 1 teaspoon minced
   fresh marjoram

2 teaspoons grated lemon
   rind
½ teaspoon pepper
1 teaspoon salt
½ teaspoon grated nutmeg
½ recipe Flaky Pastry (p. 173)

Put chicken, fat, parsley and seasonings into an electric blender. Blend for 30 seconds.

Cut the pastry into rounds with biscuit cutter. Put a spoonful of filling on one side of each round. Fold over in crescent shape. Close and crimp well.

Preheat oven to 375° F.

Bake crescents for 10 to 20 minutes, until golden brown and hot. Serve with currant jelly.

*15 rissoles*

# CHICKEN IN ASPIC

1 whole chicken, 3 to 5
   pounds
4 cups water
1 teaspoon salt
¼ teaspoon pepper

2 egg whites, slightly beaten
2 envelopes unflavored
   gelatin
lettuce
mayonnaise

Simmer chicken in 4 cups water with salt and pepper for 15 minutes. Remove breasts and continue cooking chicken until legs are done.

Remove chicken from broth and remove all bones, gristle and skin. Strain the broth.

Lay chicken meat in a glass dish in an attractive pattern of light and dark meat.

Heat the chicken broth in a saucepan; stir. Add egg whites, let boil up and then skim. Add gelatin, and stir until dissolved. Remove from heat and pour over chicken.

Cool, then refrigerate until ready to serve. Turn out onto lettuce and serve with a bowl of mayonnaise.

*6 to 8 servings*

---

# BOILED FOWL WITH OYSTER SAUCE

1 whole fowl, cleaned and
   trussed
2 quarts boiling water
¾ teaspoon salt
1 pint oysters with liquor
4 tablespoons butter

4 tablespoons flour
1¼ cups chicken stock or
   milk
¼ teaspoon pepper
2 tablespoons chopped
   parsley

Pour water over chicken, add ½ teaspoon salt, and simmer over low heat for 1½ to 2½ hours, until legs are cooked. Drain stock from fowl, and reserve. Keep fowl hot.

Cook oysters in their own liquor until the edges just curl. Remove oysters and add 1¼ cups stock from the cooked fowl.

Melt butter, add flour, and mix together into a roux; stir into the stock and oyster liquor. Add remaining salt and the pepper.

Add oysters just before ready to serve with carved fowl and rice in soup plates. Sprinkle with parsley. Serve sauce in gravy boat.

*6 to 8 servings*

---

## PLYMOUTH COLONY SUCCOTASH

This dish should be called Indian Succotash. The colonists learned how to cook corn and the rest of the ingredients to make "succototh" from the native Americans whose invention it was.

4 quarts hulled corn (hominy)
2 fowls, dressed
½ pound lean pork
2 pounds common white
    beans

1 small piece of corned beef
½ Nantucket white turnip, cut
    into small pieces
4 to 6 potatoes, sliced thin

Cook the hominy in water to cover for 4 hours, until soft.

Set fowls to cook in water to cover for 2 hours. Put pork and beans to cook in water to cover until soft, then mash.

After 2 hours skim fat from pot with fowl and add corned beef, turnip and potatoes.

When fowls are done, remove and keep hot. Remove corned beef and pork from pot when done.

Mix hominy, broth from fowl, beans and vegetables together. Serve a piece of each meat in a soup plate with vegetables.

*25 servings*

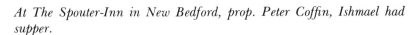

*At The Spouter-Inn in New Bedford, prop. Peter Coffin, Ishmael had supper.*

"At last some four or five of us were summoned to our meal in an adjoining room. It was cold as Iceland—no fire at all—the landlord said he couldn't afford it. Nothing but two dismal tallow candles, each in a winding sheet. We were fain to button up our monkey jackets, and hold to our lips cups of scalding tea with our half frozen fingers. But the fare was of the most substantial kind—not only meat and potatoes, but dumplings; good heavens! dumplings for supper! One young fellow in a green box coat, addressed himself to these dumplings in a most direful manner."
Moby-Dick, *Herman Melville*

## STEWED FOWL WITH DUMPLINGS

| | |
|---|---|
| 1 fowl, 4 to 5 pounds, or 2 frying chickens | ¼ teaspoon pepper |
| 2 quarts water | 5 tablespoons flour |
| ½ teaspoon salt | 1 recipe Dumplings (p. 139) |

Halve the breasts of the fowl. Bring the water to a boil. Add fowl and simmer for 2 to 3 hours, depending on tenderness of bird. Chickens require 40 minutes to 1 hour. Add salt and pepper for the last hour of cooking.

Skim off fat and reserve. Remove larger bones and cartilage, and skin if desired. Mix reserved chicken fat with flour into a roux and stir into stew.

Drop spoonfuls of dumpling dough on stew, cover, and cook for 20 minutes without lifting cover to allow dumplings to rise.

Serve in soup plates with dumplings and gravy.

*6 to 8 servings*

## BRAISED TURKEY WITH CRANBERRY STUFFING

1 turkey, 10 to 12 pounds
3 tablespoons butter
1 onion, chopped
4 cups cubed bread
½ teaspoon salt
¼ teaspoon pepper
1 teaspoon chopped fresh or
   dried sage
1 cup cranberries
1 cup water

½ pound salt pork, thinly
   sliced
3 carrots, diced
3 celery ribs, diced
3 onions, diced
1 Nantucket white turnip, or
   3 ordinary turnips, diced
½ cup each of water and
   wine

Preheat oven to 325° F.

Wipe turkey with damp cloth; remove giblets.

To make stuffing: Melt butter; sauté onion. Add bread cubes, salt, pepper and sage. Stir and mix well. Add cranberries, then sprinkle water over mixture. Remove from heat.

Stuff into turkey (do not pack) in both breast and body cavity. Tie legs of turkey together and turn breast fold over breast stuffing and under turkey. Turn wing tips under breast.

Put slices of salt pork all over breast and legs, reserving 2 slices for roasting pan. Chop the 2 slices into dice.

Put turkey in roasting pan with diced vegetables and pork, and bake for 25 minutes. Cover and cook for 1½ hours. Remove cover and allow to brown for 20 to 30 minutes.

Add ½ cup water and ½ cup wine to pan juices, stir up, and pour into gravy boat.

*10 servings*

# TO DRESS GAME BIRDS

Melt ⅜ pound of paraffin in 7 quarts of boiling water. Dip birds into and out of this mixture 4 or 5 times until feathers are well coated with paraffin. Cool until paraffin has hardened. Strip off feathers and then singe to remove pin feathers.

Chop heads and feet from birds and remove entrails. Wash in salted water.

Birds shot in the spring have strong-flavored meat, so soak in salted water with 1 tablespoon baking soda for 3 to 4 hours. This should not be necessary in the fall when chicks have fed well all summer.

Duck fanciers say that wild ducks should be dry-plucked, but it requires skill and many people prefer the paraffin method.

---

# GAME PIE

6 small birds—quails,
    pigeons, partridges or
    Cornish game hens
4 cups water
½ teaspoon salt
¼ teaspoon pepper
2 parsley sprigs
1 small onion
2 cloves
¼ pound salt pork

2 tablespoons flour
4 tablespoons butter
1 cup sliced mushrooms
2 cups diced cooked potatoes
    (optional)
1 cup full-bodied white wine
    (optional)
½ recipe Standard Pastry
    (p. 172)

Clean birds, cut into halves, and put into a frying pan. Cover with the water and bring to a boil; skim. Add salt, pepper, parsley, onion, cloves and salt pork. Simmer until birds are tender, 10 minutes if small, 20 to 30 minutes for the larger birds.

Mix flour into 2 tablespoons butter and add to pan, stirring until thickened. Cool and transfer to a casserole large enough to hold the birds.

Preheat oven to 400° F.

Sauté mushrooms in remaining butter; add to casserole. Add potatoes and wine if used.

Roll pastry to a round large enough to cover top of casserole. Cover the casserole with pastry, crimp edges, and cut vents. Bake pie for 20 to 25 minutes, until brown.

*10 to 12 servings*

---

## ROAST WILD DUCK

2 ducks, each 2½ pounds
2 onions, peeled
1 celery rib, cut into 2 pieces

1 apple, cut into 2 pieces
4 slices of salt pork

Clean ducks (see p. 81).

Stuff cavity of each duck with 1 onion, 1 piece of celery and 1 piece of apple. Cover breasts with salt pork and refrigerate overnight or all day.

Preheat oven to 500° F.

Roast ducks for 20 to 25 minutes, depending on size. Remove stuffing.

Serve duck with pan juices. (If these are mallard ducks, use only the breasts, for the legs are very tough.)

*4 servings (½ duck per person)*

*if ducks are small, 2 servings (1 per person)*

# ROAST WILD GOOSE

Canada geese migrate to and from Nantucket every year. They roost on the moors and eat berries and beach plums. In hunting season they make a fine addition to the dinner table.

| | |
|---|---|
| 1 goose | 1 onion |
| 1 teaspoon salt | butter, softened |
| ¼ teaspoon pepper | |

STUFFING

| | |
|---|---|
| 1½ cups uncooked rice | 2 tablespoons butter |
| 2½ cups water | 1 small onion, chopped |
| ½ teaspoon salt | ¼ teaspoon pepper |
| ½ cup raisins | ¼ teaspoon dried thyme |

GRAVY

| | |
|---|---|
| ½ cup wine | ½ teaspoon salt |
| ½ cup water | ¼ teaspoon pepper |

Preheat oven to 325° F.

Clean goose (see p. 81). Sprinkle with salt and pepper. Peel onion and insert in cavity. Refrigerate goose overnight.

Put rice in 2½ cups water with salt, bring to a boil, stir, half-cover, and simmer over low heat for 20 to 30 minutes, or until water is absorbed and rice is just cooked.

Cover raisins with water. Simmer for 30 minutes. Pour off and reserve cooking juice.

Melt butter in a small pan and sauté onion until golden brown. Add it and butter to rice. Add raisins, pepper and thyme to rice. Stuff into goose. Rub goose with softened butter.

Cook the bird for 20 to 25 minutes per pound, depending on size (about 2 hours), or until brown and tender. Baste once or twice.

Pour off all fat from pan, leaving brown pan drippings. Stir in raisin juice, wine and water, and salt and pepper. Serve gravy separately.

If domestic goose or duck is used with this recipe do not baste goose. Pour all fat into a coffee can; it makes wonderful cooking fat and is good for biscuits.

# BROILED QUAILS

8 quails
½ teaspoon salt
⅛ teaspoon pepper
2 small onions, peeled and
    quartered

4 slices of apple, halved
8 thin slices of salt pork
8 slices of toasted and
    buttered bread

Preheat broiler to 450° F.

Clean quails (see p. 81). Sprinkle with salt and pepper. Stuff each bird with a piece of onion and a piece of apple. Cover each with a slice of salt pork.

Broil for 8 to 12 minutes, depending on size. Serve on toast.

*4 servings*

# BROILED PHEASANT

The legs of pheasant are inclined to be tough. Some cooks prefer to use only the breast.

1 young pheasant, 1½ to 1¾
    pounds, dressed and split
1 teaspoon salt
½ teaspoon pepper

¼ pound butter, softened
3 tablespoons chopped
    parsley

Preheat oven to 500° F.

Rub pheasant halves with salt, pepper and butter. Place skin side down on broiler rack 4 inches from the source of heat, and broil for 10 to 15 minutes on each side. Brush with butter when the bird halves are turned.

Melt remaining butter; add parsley. Cover broiled birds with butter-parsley sauce just before serving.

*2 servings*

*quick*

# MEAT
# & GAME

## BOILED CORNED BEEF

Beef didn't keep before refrigeration, and it had to be salted down or pickled in brine. Brine is water with enough coarse salt in it to float an egg or a potato. The meat was immersed in the brine, weighted, and left to pickle. It could be used right away, or kept for several weeks or months, getting saltier and saltier. Each family had its own preference for the length of time the meat should be "corned"; 2 or 3 days to a week is the usual length of time.

A small amount of saltpeter may be added to the salt if desired to preserve the red color. Kosher corned beef has garlic in it, and the salt water is boiled before immersing the beef.

The cooking broth is served with boiled fresh beef, but corned beef broth is too salty.

Horseradish sauce, hot mustard, homemade ketchup and coarse salt are served as condiments with corned beef.

| | |
|---|---|
| 5 pounds corned beef | carrots |
| potatoes | cabbage |

Wash beef. Plunge into boiling water to cover. Reduce heat and skim liquid carefully as meat cooks. Cook over low heat for 3 to 4 hours.

Cut off part not wanted for use. Put in a bowl or crock and cover with the liquid in which it was cooked. Let cool in the liquid. Cover with a saucer with a weight on it. Serve later cold.

Cook potatoes and carrots in remaining liquid with the beef. Cabbage should be cut into wedges and cooked separately in boiling water for 10 minutes.

*8 to 10 servings.*

*In early Nantucket days salted beef, called "Salt Horse," was served twice a week, as was boiled salt pork. Whalemen used to say they varied their diet by having Salt Horse and Hardtack one meal, and Hardtack and Salt Horse the next, and so on . . .*

## NEW ENGLAND BOILED DINNER

This dish is the natural result of having on hand a piece of corned beef and a plentiful supply of fresh vegetables. It has, in time, been adopted by the entire nation. This recipe can also be used for fresh beef.

| | |
|---|---|
| 4 to 5 pounds corned beef in one piece | 4 or 5 turnips, peeled |
| ½ pound salt pork, scored with crisscross cuts | 6 or 7 potatoes, peeled |
| | 5 or 6 carrots |
| 5 or 6 onions | 1 head of cabbage, quartered |
| | 6 to 8 beets |

Wash the meat, place it in a large pot of boiling water with the salt pork, and simmer for 2½ to 3 hours.

Add vegetables progressively so that all are properly cooked when the meat is tender. Here is the order: First, the onions and turnips; 30 minutes later, the potatoes and carrots; 15 minutes later, the cabbage (some prefer the cabbage cooked separately). (The beets are cooked separately.) Cook for 20 minutes longer and the dinner is done.

Serve on a heated platter with the meat in the center, surrounded by the vegetables. Serve with mustard and horseradish.

*12 to 15 servings*

## GLAZED CORNED BEEF, VERMONT STYLE

Stud a hot piece of corned beef with cloves, pour on enough maple syrup to cover, and glaze in a 350° F. oven. In other parts of the country, brown sugar and mustard are substitutes for the maple syrup.

## CORNED-BEEF HASH

The best thing about corned beef is that you usually have enough left over for hash. This popular hash can be made with leftover roast beef as well.

1½ pounds corned beef, sliced
5 cold boiled potatoes, sliced
1 onion, sliced

bacon fat or cooking oil
3 tablespoons water
½ teaspoon pepper

Chop beef, potatoes and onion finely with a very sharp knife, or run them through a meat grinder. Mix together thoroughly.

Put enough bacon fat into a heavy skillet to cover the bottom, add the hash, stirring in the water, and form into a firm thin loaf. Cook slowly without stirring. Sprinkle with pepper.

When crust has developed completely, loosen hash with a spatula, fold over, and slide onto a heated platter. Cut into 4 portions, and serve each with a poached egg on top.

*4 servings*                                               *quick*

## RED FLANNEL HASH

4 medium-size potatoes, cooked and chopped
6 beets, cooked and chopped
1 cup chopped beef
2 teaspoons salt

⅛ teaspoon pepper
3 tablespoons butter
2 tablespoons water
2 tablespoons soft butter
3 tablespoons cream

Mix potatoes, beets, chopped beef, salt and pepper.

Melt 3 tablespoons butter in a skillet, add meat mixture and stir. Add 2 tablespoons water and stir. Form hash into a flat cake.

Cover and cook for 25 to 35 minutes, until there is a crust on the bottom.

Spread with soft butter, and pour on the cream. Loosen bottom crust with pancake turner and fold hash over like an omelet.

*4 servings*                                                            *quick*

---

## YANKEE POT ROAST WITH CRANBERRIES

4 to 5 pounds beef rump or
    round roast
2 tablespoons bacon fat
1 onion, peeled and diced
1 carrot, peeled, split, and
    diced

1 garlic clove, peeled and
    chopped
2 cups broth or water
1 teaspoon salt
¼ teaspoon pepper
1 cup cranberries, washed

Preheat oven to 300° F.

Brown the roast on all sides in bacon fat, about 20 minutes.

Add onion; brown slightly. Add carrot, garlic, broth, salt and pepper. Cover pan and put in oven. Cook for 2½ to 3 hours.

Skim fat from pot, and add cranberries. Simmer for 20 minutes.

Slice roast and serve in soup dishes with a bowl of gravy, boiled potatoes and horseradish mustard.

*8 servings*

---

## BEEF WITH CARROTS

4 tablespoons bacon fat
2 pounds round steak, about
    1½ inches thick
4 carrots, peeled, each cut
    into 3 pieces

½ small rutabaga, cut into
    thick slices (optional)
½ teaspoon salt
¼ teaspoon pepper

Heat bacon fat over low-medium heat. Brown round steak on one side well, then brown the other.

Add carrots and continue cooking in the same manner, turning the steak from time to time. If you use rutabaga, add slices with carrot pieces. Keep heat low. Do not add water. Add seasoning.

Serve when steak is tender, about 1 hour. Cut against the grain into thin slices. Serve carrots with the steak and a tablespoon of pan juices.

*4 servings*

## BEEF STEW WITH BURGUNDY

2 ounces salt pork, cubed, or
    6 slices of bacon
flour
2 pounds beef, chuck or
    rump, cut into 2-inch
    cubes
2 onions, sliced
1 garlic clove, crushed
1 teaspoon salt

½ teaspoon freshly ground
    pepper
2 shallots or 1 leek, chopped
½ teaspoon dried thyme
½ bay leaf
1½ cups red Burgundy wine
½ pound button mushrooms
2 or 3 ounces Cognac

Put salt pork or bacon in a heavy skillet and cook until all the fat has run out. Remove the pork pieces and save. Leave fat in skillet.

Flour the beef cubes and brown them in the pork fat along with the onions and garlic.

Season with salt and pepper, add shallots, thyme and bay leaf, and pour in the wine. Cover and simmer slowly for 3 hours, or until beef is tender.

Add mushrooms, and cook for 5 minutes longer.

Just before serving, warm the Cognac, ignite, and add flaming to the stew.

*4 servings*

# OXTAIL RAGOUT

3 oxtails, 3½ to 4 pounds
  altogether, disjointed
flour
3 cups beef stock
1 celery rib, chopped
1 carrot, chopped
1 leek, chopped

2 parsley sprigs, chopped
½ teaspoon pepper
½ teaspoon cayenne
10 whole allspice berries
1 teaspoon Worcestershire
  sauce

Dredge the oxtails with flour and put into a pot with the stock, vegetables and seasonings. Cover and stew over low heat for about 3 hours.

*6 servings*

---

# BEEF AND BARLEY HOT POT

This old Maine recipe was found in an early Rockport cookbook. We have brought it up to date and put it into the language of the modern cook.

1½ pounds beef chuck, or
  lamb or veal
2 quarts water
¾ cup uncooked pearl barley
2 teaspoons salt
1 tablespoon vinegar

2 carrots, sliced
2 onions, chopped
1 bunch of soup greens,
  washed and peeled
6 potatoes, peeled and
  quartered

Put all the ingredients into a heavy pot, cover, and cook over low heat for 2 hours, or until meat is tender.

*6 servings*

---

# NANTUCKET BEEF LOAF

2 pounds beef chuck, ground
½ cup ground salt pork
½ cup sea-biscuit crumbs
2 tablespoons finely chopped
  onion
3 eggs, beaten

½ teaspoon salt
¼ teaspoon pepper
½ teaspoon minced fresh
  sage
3 thin strips of salt pork

Preheat oven to 325° F.

Mix together the beef, salt pork, biscuit crumbs, onion, eggs and seasonings. Form into a loaf and put into a greased baking pan.

Lay the slices of salt pork across the top. Bake for 1 hour.

*4 to 6 servings*

## FLANK STEAK, PROVIDENCE STYLE

1 medium-size onion,
   chopped
2 tablespoons butter
½ flank steak, about 2
   pounds, sliced on the
   bias into ½-inch-thick
   strips

flour
1 teaspoon dry mustard
1 tablespoon vinegar
1 teaspoon salt
1 teaspoon paprika
few grains of cayenne
2 cups water

Sauté the onion in the butter in a heavy skillet.

Dredge the steak slices with flour and fry them quickly in the same skillet. Remove and set aside.

Add to the same skillet 1 tablespoon flour, the mustard, vinegar, salt, paprika and cayenne. Stir, add the water, and stir again.

Add the meat slices to the sauce, cover, and simmer for about 15 minutes.

*4 servings*                                                    *quick*

## STUFFED STEAK

This recipe from Taunton appeared in the *Boston Sunday Post,* February 18, 1906. It seemed good enough to repeat in '76.

2 pounds top round steak,
   cut thick
1 medium-size onion,
   chopped

1 teaspoon salt
½ teaspoon pepper
4 thin slices of buttered bread

Preheat oven to 400° F.

Slit steak lengthwise, leaving it closed at one edge.

Spread onion on under layer, season with salt and pepper, and lay thin slices of bread on top of this. Fold the top slice over the under slice and tie well.

Put in a buttered roasting pan and bake for 25 or 30 minutes.

*4 servings*                                                                     *quick*

## SKILLET MEAT LOAVES

1½ pounds beef, chopped
1 cup soft bread crumbs
2 tablespoons finely chopped
    onion
½ cup water or milk
1 egg, slightly beaten

1 teaspoon salt
½ teaspoon pepper
2 slices of bacon
2 tablespoons flour
⅔ cup water

Mix beef, bread crumbs, onion, ½ cup water or milk, egg, salt and pepper until well blended. Form into 4 loaves.

Fry bacon in frying pan and set aside; keep hot. Leave fat in pan.

Brown the meat loaves on both sides in the bacon fat and turn the heat to low. Cover and simmer for 25 minutes.

Remove loaves from pan to a hot platter. Stir flour into drippings in pan and let brown. Stir in ⅔ cup water until gravy is thick.

Spoon gravy on each meat loaf. Top each loaf with ½ slice of bacon and serve.

*4 servings*                                                                     *quick*

## DEVILED BEEF BONES

4 freshly roasted rib bones
salt and pepper
2 tablespoons dry mustard

3 tablespoons light cream
2 cups bread crumbs
4 tablespoons melted butter

Trim some of the fat from the rib bones, and sprinkle bones with salt and pepper.

Make a thin paste with the mustard and cream and coat the bones generously on all sides.

Sprinkle with bread crumbs, dab with melted butter, and place under the broiler until crisp, brown and crusty.

*2 to 4 servings* *quick*

---

*The following note from an old handwritten Nantucket cookbook is given verbatim: "Veal put in pan with little water salt it, put in a piece of salt pork. Bake about two hours. Beef requires no pork. Mutton like veal."*

---

## FILLED CABBAGE

This recipe feeds a number of people, about 10, and can be made on a one-burner stove or put in the oven.

| | |
|---|---|
| 1 head of cabbage, 3 to 4 pounds | 1 teaspoon grated nutmeg |
| 4 cups uncooked rice | 3 tablespoons chopped parsley |
| 4 pounds beef chuck, chopped | ½ tablespoon salt |
| 6 hot sausages, Italian sweet sausages or highly spiced sausage meat | 1 teaspoon ground rosemary |
| 1 tablespoon poultry seasoning | 2 cans (each 2 pounds) sauerkraut |
| | 1 can (2 pounds) tomatoes |

Cut core out of cabbage head and put into boiling water to cover for 4 to 5 minutes. Remove cabbage and separate leaves.

Put rice in 9 cups of water, bring to a boil, reduce heat, cover, and cook for 25 minutes, until water is absorbed.

Mix together rice, beef, sausage (removed from casings), seasoning, nutmeg, parsley, salt and rosemary. Put a good handful of this stuffing on each cabbage leaf. Fold leaves over stuffing and pin with food picks.

Lay a layer of remaining cabbage leaves on a rack in a Dutch oven. Spread a layer of half of the sauerkraut over the leaves and add half of the tomatoes. Lay the filled cabbage leaves on top of this, then another layer of sauerkraut and tomatoes. Cover all with last cabbage leaves, and cover the Dutch oven.

Cook over one burner at just a simmer for 3 hours. If oven is used, cook at 300° F. for 3 hours.

*20 cabbage leaves*

---

# WHITE VEAL STEW

White veal stew is what the Nantucketers call it, but the French, who originated the dish centuries ago, call it *blanquette de veau*. The dish is a bit of a workout, so make enough for several meals.

3 pounds shoulder or leg of
    veal, cut into 2-inch
    cubes
1 quart water
2 teaspoons salt
1 large onion, stuck with 2
    cloves
5 tablespoons chopped carrot
1 celery rib, chopped
1 bay leaf
2 sprigs of thyme

a few peppercorns
8 mushrooms
12 small white onions
5 tablespoons butter
¼ cup flour
2 egg yolks
juice of 1 lemon
6 tablespoons cream, light or
    heavy
1 teaspoon chopped parsley

Parboil the veal in a quart of salted water in a heavy saucepan; skim the scum.

Put in the onion, carrot, celery, herbs and peppercorns. Cover and simmer for 1 hour, or until meat is tender.

Boil the mushrooms in a little water for a few minutes, and cook the onions in 2 tablespoons of the butter, but do not brown.

Sauce: in a saucepan melt the remaining butter and stir in the flour, but do not brown; gradually add 2 cups of the strained stock, stirring.

Add the egg thickening made by mixing the egg yolks and lemon juice. Pour in the cream, add the veal, and simmer for a few minutes without boiling.

To serve, place the veal in a warm serving dish, pour over the sauce, and garnish with the mushrooms and onions. Sprinkle with chopped parsley.

*8 servings*

## JELLIED VEAL LOAF

2 pounds stewing veal  
1 carrot  
1 garlic clove  
1 onion, stuck with 2 cloves  
1 parsley sprig  

½ teaspoon dried thyme  
1 teaspoon salt  
¼ teaspoon pepper  
1 egg white, beaten stiff  

Cover veal with water and add all other ingredients but the egg white. Cook until very well done, about 2½ hours. Cool meat.

Strain broth into another pan. Bring broth to a boil, remove from heat, and stir in the egg white. Skim.

Chop meat and vegetables. Oil a 6-cup loaf pan, put in meat, and pour the broth over all. Refrigerate overnight.

Cut into slices, and serve on lettuce with mayonnaise.

*4 to 6 servings*

## ROAST LEG OF LAMB

1 leg of lamb, 6 pounds, skinned  
salt  

4 tablespoons brown sugar  
4 tablespoons flour  
2 tablespoons dry mustard  

Preheat oven to 350° F.

Rub lamb with salt. Make a paste by combining the sugar, flour and mustard with a little water. Cover the lamb with the paste.

Place lamb in an uncovered roasting pan and roast for about 1 hour. Add ½ cup water and reduce heat to 300° F. Cook for a total of 18 minutes per pound. (For pink lamb, cook in a 375° F. oven for 1 hour and 25 minutes.)

*"Tues. June 18, 1804, Wind southerly.*

*Arrived schooner Betsy from Cape Verde, several coasters, and the mail packet from New Bedford with a number of passengers. This is second Shearing Day.*

*It is a holiday on Nantucket, the eastern and western flocks of sheep, numbering together nearly ten thousand, were washed in Miacomet Pond on*

*Friday and Saturday of last week, and on Monday and Tuesday of this week they are publicly counted and shorn." from the Insurance Office Journal,* Quaint Nantucket, *William Root Bliss* [*These sheepshearing holidays lasted until the mid 1840s.*]

## NANTUCKET OVEN-BARBECUED LAMB

1 leg of lamb
1 tablespoon salt
flour
1 cup chopped onion
1 cup hot water

1 cup chopped cranberries
2 tablespoons sugar
4 tablespoons Worcestershire
   sauce
¼ teaspoon cayenne

Preheat oven to 450° F.

Wipe lamb dry, rub with salt, and dredge well with flour. Place on a rack in an oven pan, slide into the oven, and cook for about 30 minutes, or until well browned all over.

Reduce oven heat to 350° F. Mix all the other ingredients together and pour over the lamb.

Cook for about 20 minutes per pound, basting thoroughly every 15 minutes.

## LAMB HOT POT WITH CRANBERRIES

2 pounds lean boneless lamb,
   cut into 1-inch cubes
2 onions, sliced
1 cup cranberries
2 tablespoons sugar
5 potatoes, peeled and thinly
   sliced

1 teaspoon salt
freshly ground pepper
2 cups hot beef stock
   thickened with 1
   tablespoon flour

Preheat oven to 350° F.

In a large flameproof casserole (3-quart size) brown the meat on all sides.

Arrange layers of meat, onions, cranberries, sugar and potatoes in the pot. Season layers with salt and pepper. Continue till all ingredients are used. Top layer should be potatoes.

Pour in the beef stock, cover, and bake for 2 hours, or until meat is tender. Remove cover during last 30 minutes to brown the potatoes.

*6 servings*

# FRICASSEE OF LAMB

2 pounds stewing lamb, cut
    into 1½-inch cubes
flour
½ cup olive or other cooking
    oil
2 cups water
½ cup chopped onion

1 cup chopped carrots
3 parsley sprigs
½ bay leaf
10 peppercorns
2 cloves
2 teaspoons salt

Remove excess fat from lamb. Flour the cubes and brown on all sides in hot oil in a heavy pot.

Put all the remaining ingredients into the pot, cover, and cook over low heat for about 2 hours, or until meat is tender. Thin with additional water if necessary.

*6 servings*

# STUFFED LAMB SHANKS

4 lamb shanks
2 tablespoons butter
3 cups water
1 teaspoon salt

¼ teaspoon pepper
1 cup uncooked barley
flour

Brown the lamb shanks on all sides in the butter in a heavy skillet.

Add the water, seasonings and barley. Cover and simmer for 1½ hours, or until lamb is tender, adding water as needed. Remove the meat, cool, and take out the bones.

Continue to cook the barley in the lamb broth for about 30 minutes longer. Stuff barley into boned shanks.

Thicken the gravy with a little flour-water mixture and pour over the shanks. Cover, heat for 15 minutes, and serve.

*4 servings*                                                    *make ahead*

## MULLIGAN STEW WITH DUMPLINGS

Mulligan stew differs from most other stews in that the meat is never floured or browned before cooking and the gravy is not thickened. For this last reason, the stew is often served with dumplings.

2 pounds stewing lamb
⅛ pound salt pork, cubed
2 cups water
½ cup diced carrot
½ cup diced turnip
½ cup chopped celery
½ cup sliced onion
4 potatoes, peeled and
    quartered

1 teaspoon salt
½ teaspoon whole
    peppercorns
1 cup flour
2 teaspoons baking powder
½ teaspoon salt
½ cup milk

Simmer the lamb and salt pork in 2 cups water for 30 minutes.

Add the vegetables and seasonings and simmer slowly for 1 hour.

Mix together the flour, baking powder, salt and milk, and drop by the spoonful onto the boiling stew. Cook for about 12 minutes.

*4 servings*

---

## BOSTON IRISH STEW

3 pounds stewing lamb
12 medium-size potatoes, peeled
4 or 5 onions, sliced

pinch of thyme
salt and pepper
2 cups water

Remove the fat from the meat, and cut meat into pieces. Use the bones to get extra flavor.

Slice half the potatoes thinly, leaving the rest whole.

Put everything except the whole potatoes into a large pot, season well, and add 2 cups of water. Cover the pot and simmer for 1½ hours.

Toss in the whole potatoes, cover, and simmer for another hour, or until potatoes are done. The thinly sliced potatoes dissolve and thicken the stew while the whole potatoes retain their shape.

*about 6 servings*

## ROAST LOIN OF PORK, CRANBERRY GLAZE

7 to 8 pounds loin of pork,
  center cut or loin end
1 teaspoon salt
¼ teaspoon pepper

8 sweet potatoes, peeled
½ cup sugar
1 cup cranberries
1 cup water

Preheat oven to 325° F.

Wipe pork loin with damp cloth. Sprinkle with half the salt and pepper and put in open baking pan. Roast for 2 hours.

Add peeled potatoes after first 30 minutes of roasting. Turn potatoes once or twice.

Cook sugar and cranberries together for about 10 minutes, until sauce is thick and berries have burst.

Remove potatoes from roasting pan and keep hot. Spread cranberry glaze over pork loin and return to oven until roast is glazed, about 10 to 15 minutes. Remove loin from pan and place on a hot platter.

Add remaining salt and pepper to pan and 1 cup water. Stir and pour into gravy boat. Serve with potatoes.

*8 servings*

## PORTUGUESE PORK CHOPS WITH CLAMS

4 large pork chops
12 Little Neck clams
1 tablespoon chopped onion

1 garlic clove, chopped
½ teaspoon salt
¼ teaspoon pepper

Brown pork chops in frying pan for about 15 minutes on each side.

Scrub clam shells well with a brush. Wash in several waters. Discard any with open shells. Drain.

Add onion, garlic, salt and pepper to pan with the pork chops. Stir. Add clams. Cover pan and cook just until clam shells open. Serve with rice.

*4 servings*                                                    *quick*

*Featured on the menu of a whaleship:* Lob Scouse, *a stew of soaked hardtack, pork fat, or top of the pot (grease left after boiling beef), or any sort of "slush" (sailor's term for grease), boiled with molasses and water.*

*Potato Scouse was the same as above excepting that potatoes were substituted for hardtack.*

## PORK WITH HULLED CORN

This recipe, a variety of succotash, came from an old notebook; we reprint it just as it originally appeared.

"Put water on quite early, when boiling, put in the corn and let boil all the forenoon. Parboil the beans and put them in. Parboil the pork put that in. To 2 pints? of corn ½ pint beans."

In winter this was made with dried corn and dried pea beans bought at the seed store. We made it with country-style spareribs, onion, fresh corn and lima beans. It is an excellent dish with a real country flavor.

2 to 3 pounds country-style
    spareribs or loin-end
    pork loin
1 onion, sliced
1 pound fresh lima beans in
    shell, or 1 package (10
    ounces) frozen beans

6 ears of fresh corn, cut off
    cobs
1 teaspoon salt
¼ teaspoon pepper

Put pork on to boil in water to cover. When it boils, skim, reduce heat, add onion, and simmer pork until tender, about 1½ hours.

Shell fresh beans and add after 1 hour of cooking. If beans are frozen, add with corn. Add corn 15 minutes before serving. Add seasoning.

*4 to 6 servings*

## SALT PORK WITH CREAM SAUCE

1½ pounds salt pork, thinly
    sliced

3 cups milk
flour

Soak the salt pork in 1 cup milk for 2 hours. Dry and dredge with flour. Fry until crisp. Remove slices to heated platter. Reserve 2 tablespoons fat from pork.

Heat the fat in a heavy skillet. Sift in 3 tablespoons flour and stir in 2 cups milk; stir constantly until thickened to desired consistency. Pour over the salt pork.

*4 servings*

## HAM HASH

1 pound boiled lean ham,
    finely chopped
2 eggs

½ teaspoon salt
½ teaspoon pepper
2 tablespoons butter

Mix ham, eggs, salt and pepper.

Melt butter in frying pan, add ham mixture, and flatten into a cake. Cook for 2 minutes on one side, turn, and cook on other side.

Serve with hot biscuits.

*2 servings*

*quick*

# SAUSAGE CAKES

Sausage meat was chopped with a sharp knife on a board, or in a wooden chopping bowl with a sharp two-bladed chopper, before meat grinders were invented. In New England, this method is still preferred.

2 pounds raw lean pork or
    beef
1 pound salt pork
1 tablespoon pepper

3 tablespoons chopped fresh
    sage, or 1½ tablespoons
    dried sage

Cut fresh pork or beef and salt pork into small pieces. Chop fine in chopping bowl or board with sharp cook's knife or cleaver. Mix well.

Add pepper and sage and mix well. Make into small flat cakes. Fry on a hot dry skillet for 5 to 7 minutes on each side.

*16 small cakes*

# CHITLINS AND BRITCHES

Chitterlings, called chitlins in Nantucket as in the South, are the intestines of the pig. Britches (breeches) are fresh cod roe, a pair of which resemble a pair of breeches. Put them together and you have an early Nantucket dish often served for breakfast.

1 pound chitterlings, cleaned
¼ cup vinegar
1 pound cod roe
1 egg

½ teaspoon salt
2 tablespoons water
½ cup cracker crumbs
bacon fat or lard

Wash chitterlings carefully and soak in water to cover with vinegar. Peel off lining, leaving a little fat. Cut into 1½-inch pieces. Wipe roe gently with a damp cloth. Do not break skin.

Beat egg; add salt and water. Dip chitterlings and roe into beaten egg mixture. Roll in cracker crumbs.

Melt fat in frying pan until just smoking (365° F.). Fry roe until golden brown. Fry chitterlings until golden. Drain on brown paper.

*4 servings*                                                           *quick*

## RABBIT STEW WITH WINE

Rabbits these days are cultivated for sale fresh in city markets, or sold dressed and frozen in convenient packages. The wild rabbits found on Nantucket require soaking in salted, vinegared water for 2 hours before cooking.

3 pounds rabbit, fresh or
    frozen
flour
2 tablespoons bacon fat
1 onion, sliced
1 cup water

1 cup dry white wine
½ teaspoon salt
¼ teaspoon pepper
pinch of sweet basil
pinch of marjoram
chopped parsley

Have the rabbit dressed and cut up.

Dredge the parts with flour, and brown them on all sides in hot bacon fat in a heavy skillet.

Add the onion, water, wine, seasonings, and basil and marjoram. Cover and simmer for about 1 hour, or until rabbit is tender when fork-tested.

Thicken the sauce, if desired, with 1 tablespoon flour dissolved in ¼ cup water. Cook until thickened. Sprinkle with chopped parsley and serve.

*4 servings*

## VERMONT RABBIT STEW

1 pair rabbits
3 slices of salt pork, diced
4 tablespoons flour
1 tablespoon butter
2 onions, chopped

2 sprigs of fresh thyme, or ½
    teaspoon dried thyme
2 cups chicken broth
3 tablespoons chopped
    parsley

Skin, wash, cut up rabbits. Soak in salted water overnight. If rabbit is not available use the same weight of second joints of chicken. Do not soak chicken.

Put salt pork in a frying pan over low heat. Roll pieces of rabbit in flour.

Add butter to pan; when hot add pieces of rabbit. Cook on one side for 10 minutes, turn, and cook on the other. Add onions and thyme. Cook until onions are light brown.

Add broth and parsley. Cook for 35 to 40 minutes, or until rabbits are tender.

*6 to 8 servings*

---

## BAKED VENISON

Venison is a very lean meat and should be larded or cooked with strips of pork fat. What venison fat there is should always be trimmed away since it tends to cling unpleasantly to the roof of the mouth.

| | |
|---|---|
| 1 haunch or saddle of venison, trimmed and washed | ½ carrot, chopped |
| | 1 tablespoon chopped parsley |
| | ½ teaspoon salt |
| 1 cup red wine | ⅛ teaspoon pepper |
| 1 onion, chopped | ¼ pound salt pork, sliced |

Put venison into a bowl with wine, onion, carrot, parsley, salt and pepper. Refrigerate overnight.

Preheat oven to 325° F.

Remove venison from marinade and dry; reserve marinade. Put venison in baking pan, and cover with thin slices of salt pork.

Bake for 10 minutes to the pound. A large haunch requires about 1½ hours; a doe, or small haunch, about 1 hour. Venison should be pink, not overdone.

Remove haunch from pan. Strain marinade, and add to pan juices. Let boil up. Serve in gravy boat.

*8 to 12 servings*

# VENISON STEAK

4 venison steaks, 1 to 1½
   inches thick
3 tablespoons olive oil
1 garlic clove, halved
½ teaspoon salt

¼ teaspoon pepper
4 slices of bacon
¾ cup of half wine, half
   water

Remove all fat from venison. Marinate steaks in mixture of oil, garlic, salt and pepper, turning the steaks once or twice in mixture. Cover and refrigerate until ready to cook.

Cook bacon in heavy frying pan; remove and keep hot.

Brown steaks for 7 minutes on each side for medium-rare, slightly longer for pink venison. Put venison on a serving plate with a piece of bacon on each steak.

Swirl cooking pan with wine and water to deglaze, and serve this pan sauce separately in a small bowl.

Mushrooms sautéed in butter for 5 minutes are an excellent accompaniment to this steak. So is Grape Ketchup (p. 184).

*4 servings*

# VEGETABLES &
# SIDE DISHES

## GARLIC ARTICHOKES

This unusual recipe came highly recommended from a native Nantucketer. Never having found the dish in any other part of the country, we must conclude that it is truly a native delicacy.

4 medium-size artichokes    ½ cup oil
4 garlic cloves, peeled    ½ cup chicken soup

Remove the chokes and bruised large outer leaves from the artichokes and cut off the stems. Insert a garlic clove in the center of each artichoke and arrange in a baking pan with lid.

Pour over the oil and then the soup, cover tightly, and cook over low heat for 1 hour.

*4 servings*

---

## FRIED ASPARAGUS

12 cooked fresh or canned    fine bread crumbs
   asparagus tips    fat for deep-frying
1 egg, lightly beaten    salt and pepper

Wipe the asparagus dry. Dip into the egg, then into the bread crumbs. Fry a few at a time in fat heated to 380° F. for 2 or 3 minutes, or until golden. Season to taste and serve.

*2 or 3 servings* *quick*

---

## NEW ENGLAND BAKED BEANS

2 pounds dried navy beans, soaked overnight
½ pound salt pork
½ cup sugar

½ cup molasses
2 teaspoons dry mustard
1 teaspoon salt
2 cups cooking water, boiling

Preheat oven to 300° F.

Parboil the beans until skins crack open. Drain; reserve cooking water; measure out 2 cups. Put beans into a 4-quart bean pot.

Score the salt pork with deep crisscross cuts down to the rind and place on top of the beans.

Mix together the sugar, molasses, mustard, salt and reserved 2 cups water, and pour over the beans.

Bake for about 6 hours, adding more of reserved water as it becomes necessary to keep beans moist.

*16 servings*

---

## PORTUGUESE BAKED BEANS

2 cups dried navy beans
2 tablespoons bacon fat
2 garlic cloves, finely chopped
2 tomatoes, chopped

1 large onion, sliced
2 thick slices of bacon or salt pork, diced

Preheat oven to 250° F.

Soak navy beans in water to cover overnight. Drain and reserve soaking water.

Melt bacon fat over low heat; add garlic, tomatoes and onion. Cook for 5 minutes, then add beans and diced bacon.

Transfer to 2-quart bean pot or casserole and add bean water to bring level barely to level of beans. Bake for 5½ to 6 hours. Add additional water as necessary to keep water at level. Serve with Johnny Cake.

*8 servings*

# HARVARD BEETS

1 teaspoon cornstarch
½ cup sugar
¼ cup vinegar
¼ cup water
8 to 10 small beets, cooked,
    peeled and cubed, or 1
    pound canned beets

1 teaspoon salt
½ teaspoon pepper
3 tablespoons butter

Put the cornstarch, sugar, vinegar and water into a saucepan, and boil for a few minutes.

Remove from the heat, add the beets, and allow to stand for about 1 hour.

Season with salt and pepper, add the butter, bring to a quick boil, and serve.

*4 servings*                                                      *quick*

# BAKED BROCCOLI WITH CHEESE

1 pound fresh or frozen
    chopped broccoli
1 egg, lightly beaten
1 cup milk
½ cup creamed cottage
    cheese

juice of ½ lemon
1 teaspoon salt
½ teaspoon pepper
½ teaspoon grated nutmeg

Cook the broccoli in a little salted water for 5 minutes, or until almost tender but not soft. Drain, chop coarsely, and transfer to a buttered casserole.

Preheat oven to 325° F.

Mix together the egg, milk, cheese, lemon juice and seasonings. Pour over the broccoli. Bake for about 30 minutes, or until custard is firm.

*4 to 6 servings* *quick*

## SCALLOPED CABBAGE

1 small cabbage
4 tablespoons butter
½ cup chopped celery
2 tablespoons flour
1 cup half-and-half milk and
  cream

½ teaspoon chopped fresh
  dill
2 teaspoons salt
½ teaspoon pepper
bread crumbs

Remove the outer leaves from the cabbage, cut head into quarters, remove the tough center, and slice leaves into shreds. Cook in boiling water for 5 to 10 minutes, or until tender. Drain.

Preheat oven to 350° F.

Melt 2 tablespoons of the butter in a 4- to 6-cup casserole, add the celery, and cook over low heat for 5 minutes. Stir in the flour and then the half-and-half. Cook for about 5 minutes longer, or until sauce is thickened.

Add the cabbage and seasonings. Cover with bread crumbs, dot with remaining butter, and bake until brown on top.

*4 servings*

## VERMONT CANDIED CARROTS

1 pound carrots, washed and
  scrubbed
¼ pound butter

½ teaspoon salt
½ cup maple syrup
¼ teaspoon grated nutmeg

If carrots are old, scrape them too. Cut the carrots lengthwise into halves, or quarters if large.

Melt the butter in a heavy skillet; add carrots and salt, and cook for 15 minutes.

Stir in the maple syrup and nutmeg, and cook over low heat until well glazed.

*4 servings*                                                              *quick*

## CAULIFLOWER AU GRATIN

1 whole cauliflower, washed,
   with leaves and stalk
   removed
3 tablespoons butter
3 tablespoons flour
1 teaspoon salt

½ teaspoon pepper
1 cup milk
1 cup grated mild Cheddar
   cheese
½ cup bread crumbs

Cook the cauliflower in boiling salted water for 15 minutes. Drain and transfer to a casserole. (If desired, cauliflower can be broken into flowerets before cooking.)

Melt 2 tablespoons of the butter in a small saucepan, stir in the flour, salt and pepper and then the milk, continuing to stir until sauce is thickened.

Pour the cream sauce over the cauliflower. Sprinkle on the cheese, then the bread crumbs. Dot with remaining butter and bake for 10 to 15 minutes, or until browned.

*4 servings*                                                              *quick*

## BRAISED CELERY

2 bunches of celery, washed
   and quartered, with
   leaves removed
1 cup chicken broth or salted
   water

1 tablespoon butter
½ cup light cream
½ teaspoon grated nutmeg
½ teaspoon salt
½ teaspoon pepper

Place the celery in a skillet with the broth, and cook for 15 to 20 minutes, or until tender.

Remove the celery to a heated dish. Add the butter, cream and nutmeg to the liquid in the skillet. Stir and pour over the celery. Season with salt and pepper and serve.

*4 servings*

# FIDDLEHEADS

Bracken or ostrich ferns should be picked in the very early spring. Pick the fronds about 6 inches high, the part that snaps easily, before veil turns yellow. Pick from several plants so that the plants will not die. The fronds look like little curled fiddleheads, hence the name.

| | |
|---|---|
| 1 pound fresh or frozen fiddleheads | 2 tablespoons butter |
| 1 tablespoon vinegar | 1 teaspoon salt |
| | ⅛ teaspoon pepper |

Wash fresh fiddleheads and remove veil.

Drop into boiling water to cover and cook for 20 to 30 minutes, or until tender. Drain.

Add vinegar, butter, salt and pepper, and serve.

*4 to 6 servings*                                                    *quick*

---

# CORN ON THE COB, INDIAN STYLE

Select fresh young corn, and remove the outer husks. Peel back the inner husks but do not remove them. Clean away the "silk," then fold the inner husks back into place. Simmer in salted water until just tender; too much cooking will toughen the corn.   *quick*

---

# CORN OYSTERS

These fritters can be served for breakfast, lunch, or as an accompaniment to meat for dinner.

| | |
|---|---|
| 2 cups grated green corn, 4 to 5 well-filled ears | 3 tablespoons milk (if needed) |
| 1 cup flour | 1 teaspoon salt |
| 5 tablespoons melted butter | ⅛ teaspoon pepper |
| 1 egg, beaten | |

Mix all together and drop in small pancakes into a buttered pan. Fry until golden brown on both sides. If corn is very young and milky, the 3 tablespoons of milk will not be needed.

*6 servings*                                                         *quick*

## CORN PUDDING

| | |
|---|---|
| 2 cups corn kernels, fresh green or cream-style canned | 1 cup milk |
| | 2 eggs, separated, well beaten |
| | 1 teaspoon salt |
| 4 tablespoons butter | ½ teaspoon pepper |
| 4 tablespoons crushed common crackers or sea toast | |

Preheat oven to 350° F.

Corn should be cut from cobs and the cut cobs scraped into bowl.

Melt 2 tablespoons of the butter in a heavy casserole. Stir in the crackers; add the milk, corn, beaten egg yolks and seasonings, and stir.

Fold in the beaten egg whites, dot with the remaining butter, and bake for 30 minutes.

*4 to 6 servings*

## DANDELION GREENS

The nuisance weed of everybody's lawn can make a delicious dish, but only if you work fast. Dandelions are only tender enough for eating briefly after they first appear in the Spring. When they bloom, it's too late—too tough. Add them to other greens for extra flavor in salads or serve as a vegetable course. This recipe can be used also for mustard greens, chicory, turnip tops and other greens.

| | |
|---|---|
| 3 pounds fresh young dandelions, washed and coarsely chopped | 1 cup water |
| | 1 teaspoon pepper |
| | 2 tablespoons butter |
| 3 teaspoons salt | ½ cup chopped crisp bacon |

Sprinkle the greens with 2 teaspoons salt and put into a pot with the water. Cover and cook for 10 minutes, or until barely tender.

Drain. Season with 1 teaspoon each of salt and pepper, stir in the butter and bacon bits, and serve.

*4 servings*                                    *quick*

## BAKED STUFFED EGGPLANT

1 medium-size eggplant,
   about 1 pound
2 cups bread crumbs
1 egg, well beaten
½ cup minced onion

1 tablespoon bacon fat
1 teaspoon salt
few grains of cayenne
1 tablespoon butter

Cook the eggplant in boiling salted water for 15 minutes.

Drain. Cut eggplant lengthwise into halves and remove the pulp, taking care not to break the skin.

Chop the pulp; mix well with 1 cup of the bread crumbs, the egg, onion and bacon fat. Season with salt and cayenne.

Preheat oven to 375° F.

Pile the stuffing mixture into the eggplant halves, sprinkle with the remaining bread crumbs, and dot with butter. Bake for about 30 minutes.

*4 servings*

---

## STUFFED MUSHROOMS

Mushrooms can be found growing wild in the fields of Nantucket and much of New England, but unless one is an experienced picker it is safer to buy them in the market.

12 large fresh mushrooms,
   washed and dried
4 tablespoons butter
½ tablespoon minced onion
2 tablespoons flour
2 tablespoons heavy cream

½ cup minced ham
1 teaspoon minced parsley
1 teaspoon salt
few grains of cayenne
bread crumbs

Preheat oven to 400° F.

Remove the stems from the mushrooms. Chop stems and sauté them in the butter along with the onion for 10 minutes.

Stir in the flour, cream, ham, parsley and seasonings, and pile onto the inverted mushroom caps. Sprinkle with bread crumbs and bake for 15 minutes.

*4 servings*                                        *quick*

## MUSHROOMS WITH HAM

1 pound fresh mushrooms
2 tablespoons butter
2 slices of ham, chopped

1 cup sour cream
4 slices of toast, buttered

Wash and trim mushrooms.

Melt butter in a skillet with a cover, put in the mushrooms, and sauté over low-medium heat for 5 minutes. Shake the pan from time to time.

Add the ham and the sour cream. Stir. Heat for 5 minutes longer and serve on hot toast.

*4 servings*                                                                                              *quick*

## SCALLOPED POTATOES WITH ONION

4 raw potatoes, peeled and
    thinly sliced
1 onion, thinly sliced
1 teaspoon salt

½ teaspoon pepper
2 tablespoons flour
4 tablespoons melted butter
1½ cups milk, approximately

Preheat oven to 350° F.

Put a layer of some of the potatoes, onion, seasonings, flour and butter into a casserole. Repeat until 3 layers are formed.

Add enough milk barely to reach to level of potatoes. Bake for 1 hour or more, or until potatoes are tender.

*4 servings*

## SKILLET-FRIED POTATOES

4 medium-size potatoes
3 tablespoons bacon fat

¼ teaspoon salt
⅛ teaspoon pepper

Peel potatoes and slice about ¼ inch thick.

Melt fat in skillet. Add potatoes. Spread them in a layer over the skillet. Cover and cook over medium heat for 5 minutes.

When potatoes are brown turn and spread out in layers. Cover, and cook until brown on the bottom. Reduce heat and cook until the slices are tender. Sprinkle with salt and pepper.

*4 servings*                                                                 *quick*

## SCALLION AND HAM PIE

2 cups sliced scallions or
    spring onions
3 tablespoons butter
1 cup diced cooked ham
pastry for 1-crust 8-inch pie,
    unbaked (p. 172)

2 eggs, lightly beaten
½ cup light cream
1 teaspoon salt
½ teaspoon pepper

Sauté the scallions in the butter until tender. Add the ham and cook for a few minutes longer.

Preheat oven to 400° F.

Line an 8-inch pie pan with the pastry. Crimp edges.

Spoon the scallions and ham into the pastry. Mix together the eggs, cream and seasonings, and spoon over the scallion-ham mixture.

Bake for about 20 minutes, or until firm.

*4 servings*

## SUMMER SQUASH CASSEROLE

1½ pounds fresh young
    squash, cleaned and
    sliced
1 large onion, sliced

¼ pound butter
1 teaspoon salt
½ teaspoon pepper
½ cup heavy cream

Preheat oven to 400° F.

Place the squash and onion slices into a buttered casserole, dot with butter, and season with salt and pepper. Cover and bake for 30 minutes.

Uncover, add the cream, and bake for 10 minutes longer, or until golden brown.

*4 servings*                                                                 *quick*

## CRANBERRIED SWEET POTATOES

¼ pound butter
½ cup sugar
½ cup chopped cranberries

4 boiled sweet potatoes,
   peeled and cut
   lengthwise into 1-inch-
   thick slices

Heat the butter, sugar and cranberries in a heavy skillet and add the potatoes. Cook, turning, until delicately brown on both sides.

*4 servings*                                                                    *quick*

## DEVILED TOMATOES

4 small, or 2 large, unpeeled
   tomatoes, cut into halves
1 tablespoon minced onion
⅛ teaspoon dried orégano
6 tablespoons butter
2 teaspoons sugar

1 egg, lightly beaten
1 tablespoon vinegar
1 teaspoon dry mustard
½ teaspoon salt
few grains of cayenne

Preheat oven broiler to 350° F.

Place the tomatoes, cut sides up, in a shallow broiling pan. Sprinkle with onion and orégano, and dot with 1 tablespoon of butter. Broil for 6 to 8 minutes. Remove to a heated platter.

Put the remaining ingredients into a saucepan and cook-stir over very low heat until thickened. Pour the sauce over the tomatoes and serve.

*4 servings*                                                                    *quick*

## NANTUCKET WHITE TURNIP

1 Nantucket white turnip, 1
   pound
4 tablespoons butter

½ teaspoon salt
⅛ teaspoon pepper

Grate turnip. Add butter, salt and pepper, and cook all together until turnip is tender, about 20 minutes.

*4 servings*                                                                    *quick*

## MASHED NANTUCKET TURNIP

1 Nantucket white turnip, 1½      ½ teaspoon pepper
     pounds                   ½ cup heavy cream, whipped
1 teaspoon salt

Wash and pare the turnip, and slice. Cook in boiling water for about 20 minutes, or until tender.

Drain, mash, and season with salt and pepper. Fold in the whipped cream, warm, and serve.

*4 servings*                                                *quick*

## ITALIAN FRIED ZUCCHINI

4 medium-size zucchini         flour
½ teaspoon salt                 ½ cup olive oil

Wash, but do not peel zucchini. Cut lengthwise into quarters. Remove center pulp and seeds from the zucchini.

Cut zucchini quarters into pieces the size of French fried potatoes. Sprinkle with salt. Let stand for 15 minutes to draw the juice from the zucchini. Drain, dry, and roll in flour.

Heat oil in frying pan. Fry zucchini in oil until brown. Drain on brown paper and serve immediately.

*4 to 6 servings*                                     *quick*

*"April 30th Tues.*

*As there was no newspaper on the island, the night-watchman, tramping his rounds, became an advertising herald, announcing with the hours the wares that are to be sold by his customers tomorrow. Hear him: 'Twelve o'clock. All is well. Jabez Arey has beans to sell.' " from Insurance Office Journal,* Quaint Nantucket, *William Root Bliss*

# SALADS

## BOSTON BAKED BEAN SALAD

3 cups cold baked beans
1 cup finely chopped onion
1 green pepper, finely
    chopped

1 tablespoon sugar
½ teaspoon salt
¼ cup wine vinegar
½ cup olive oil

Mix together all the ingredients, chill, and serve on lettuce.

*4 servings*

---

## MASSACHUSETTS GREEN AND YELLOW
## BEAN SALAD

4 cups cut-up green and
    yellow beans
1 tablespoon finely chopped
    onion
4 tablespoons olive oil
½ teaspoon salt

¼ teaspoon pepper
1½ tablespoons vinegar
1 teaspoon dried thyme, or 1
    sprig of fresh thyme,
    chopped
½ cup chopped green pepper

Cook beans until tender. Drain.

Mix onion, oil, salt, pepper, vinegar, thyme and green pepper. Add to beans. Refrigerate for several hours.

*6 to 8 servings*

## BROCCOLI VINAIGRETTE

1 bunch of broccoli
4 cups boiling water
1 teaspoon salt
½ teaspoon pepper

¼ cup olive oil
1 tablespoon vinegar
1 tablespoon chopped capers
1 tablespoon chopped parsley

Break broccoli head into flowerets. Peel stalk and cut into bite-size pieces.

Drop into 4 cups boiling water in a large frying pan and cook uncovered for 20 minutes, or until tender. Drain. Cool.

Mix salt, pepper, oil, vinegar, capers and parsley. Rub through a sieve.

Arrange drained broccoli in a bowl. Spoon the vinaigrette over it. Let marinate until ready to serve. Or serve in individual bowls.

*6 to 8 servings*

## CATTAIL SALAD

Cattails, those tall reeds that grow in wet soil and around ponds, are prolific on Nantucket. Young cattails are pulled up singly by the roots, and peeled. About 3 to 4 inches of the lower stem is eaten. Cattails are crisp and have a delicate flavor like water chestnuts. They can be used very nicely in conjunction with other greens in salads.

1 head of romaine
16 cattails, peeled, and
    trimmed to white part
3 ounces cream cheese

1 cup mayonnaise
2 tablespoons heavy cream
1 teaspoon chopped chives

Wash and dry romaine. Remove the tougher outer leaves and save for another use. Keep inner leaves intact and divide into 4 servings, graduating the leaves from inside to out for each serving. Add 4 cattails. Put in refrigerator to crisp.

Mix cheese, mayonnaise, cream and chives. Spoon onto 4 salad plates.

The leaves and cattails are picked up with the fingers and dipped into the dressing.

*4 servings*                                                            *quick*

## OLD-FASHIONED CHICKEN SALAD

1 whole chicken
2 hard-cooked eggs
¼ cup vinegar
1 teaspoon butter, softened
1 teaspoon dry mustard

½ teaspoon black pepper
½ teaspoon salt
½ teaspoon minced fresh
    thyme
lettuce

Simmer chicken until done, about 15 minutes for breast, 30 minutes for dark meat. Remove all bones, gristle and skin. Chop chicken into bite-size pieces.

Chop hard-cooked eggs. Mix in vinegar, butter, mustard, pepper, salt and thyme. Mix in the chicken and serve on chilled lettuce.

*4 to 6 servings*

## NEW ENGLAND CORNED-BEEF SALAD

2 cups cubed cooked corned
    beef
1 cup chopped celery
½ cup chopped stuffed olives
½ cup chopped onion
1 teaspoon salt

2 tablespoons French
    dressing
lettuce
2 hard-cooked eggs, chopped
mayonnaise or other dressing
paprika

Mix together the corned beef, celery, olives, onion, salt and 2 tablespoons dressing.

Pile onto lettuce leaves, and sprinkle with chopped egg. Top with mayonnaise or your favorite dressing, and dust with paprika.

*4 servings*                                                    *quick*

## DANDELION SALAD

In early spring before the dandelions bloom, pick the leaves and make them into a salad.

4 hard-cooked eggs
3 tablespoons olive oil
½ teaspoon salt
1 teaspoon prepared
    mustard

⅛ teaspoon pepper
1 tablespoon lemon juice
1½ to 2 pounds fresh
    dandelion greens

Chop hard-cooked eggs. Add oil, salt, mustard, pepper and lemon juice. Stir.

Pick over, trim, and wash greens. Dry well, tear into bite-size pieces, and refrigerate.

When ready to serve arrange greens in a bowl, pour on the dressing, and toss.

*4 to 6 servings*                                                  *quick*

## NEW ENGLAND COLESLAW

| | |
|---|---|
| 4 cups shredded cabbage | 2 tablespoons vinegar |
| ½ cup julienned carrot | 1 cup mayonnaise |
| ½ cup julienned green | ½ cup light sweet cream |
|    pepper | 1 teaspoon celery seeds |
| 1 tablespoon sugar | 1 teaspoon salt |
| ½ teaspoon dry mustard | ½ teaspoon pepper |

Mix together all the ingredients, chill, and serve.

*4 to 6 servings*                                                  *quick*

## HOT COLESLAW

| | |
|---|---|
| 2 eggs, lightly beaten | ¼ cup water |
| 1 teaspoon sugar | ½ teaspoon salt |
| 1 tablespoon butter | ½ head of cabbage, shredded |
| ¼ cup vinegar | |

Mix together the eggs, sugar, butter, vinegar, water and salt in the top compartment of a double boiler, stirring until thickened.

Add the shredded cabbage, stir for a few minutes, and serve.

*4 servings*                                                  *quick*

# CRANBERRIES

The cranberry is a low, creeping plant that thrives in boggy, spongy soil composed mainly of sand and decayed vegetable matter. It is found along the coastal areas of New England and New

Jersey, and in lake regions of Wisconsin. Some of the largest bogs in the world are said to be in Nantucket.

Nowadays cranberries are cultivated in their natural habitat, the nurtured berries destined for commercial distribution being required to pass "the bouncing test." They must bounce seven times, landing on the other side of a 4-inch-high barrier.

Cranberries keep well. This combined with an unusual tart-bitter flavor makes them a very versatile food, usable in almost any kind of dish from soup to nuts.

In Sweden there is a smaller cousin of the cranberry known as the lingonberry, equally popular gastronomically.

## CRANBERRY ASPIC

1 envelope unflavored
   gelatin, dissolved in
   1 cup warm bouillon
1 cup cranberries
½ cup chopped celery

grated rind of ½ orange
   (zest)
½ cup sugar
½ cup claret

Put all the ingredients into an electric blender and blend until smooth.

Pour into an oiled 3-cup ring or other mold, and chill until firm. Turn out onto a bed of chilled lettuce and serve.

*4 servings*

## MOLDED CRANBERRY SALAD

1½ cups cranberries, washed
rind of ½ orange (zest)
½ cup sugar
1 cup orange juice

1 envelope unflavored
   gelatin, dissolved in ½
   cup boiling water
½ cup chopped celery

Put the cranberries and orange rind through a meat grinder. Add the sugar and allow to stand for an hour or so.

Add the orange juice, gelatin solution and celery. Pour into a 3½- or 4-cup mold. Chill. Serve on lettuce, topped with mayonnaise.

*6 to 8 servings*

## HALIBUT SALAD

2 halibut or other fish fillets
½ teaspoon salt
1 celery rib, finely chopped
1 pimiento, finely chopped

¼ cup mayonnaise
¼ teaspoon pepper
lettuce
chopped parsley

Simmer fillets in salted water until just done. Cool. Flake fish, removing all skin and bones. Feel flakes with fingers to make sure.

Add celery, pimiento, mayonnaise and pepper; stir. Pack into 4 individual molds or custard cups, 6- to 8-ounce size.

Serve on lettuce. Sprinkle with chopped parsley.

*4 servings*                                                                       *quick*

## LENTIL SALAD, VINAIGRETTE

2 cups dried lentils
1 quart water
4 tablespoons olive oil
1 tablespoon vinegar
1 teaspoon finely chopped
    onion

2 tablespoons capers,
    chopped
lettuce

Pick over and wash lentils and put in 1 quart water. Cook until soft, but not mushy, about 1½ hours. They will have absorbed most of the water. Drain and cool.

Mix together the other ingredients except lettuce and add to lentils. Toss. Serve on lettuce.

*12 servings*

## MAINE LOBSTER SALAD

4 lobsters, 1¼ pounds each,
    cooked and cooled
French dressing
few grains of cayenne

1 cup finely chopped celery
1½ cups mayonnaise
paprika
4 slices of lemon

Carefully remove the meat from the lobsters, leaving the shells intact.

Cut the meat into neat pieces. Sprinkle with French dressing and cayenne, cover, and refrigerate for about 1 hour.

Mix the lobster with the celery and mayonnaise. Pile it back into the shells. Dust with paprika and serve with lemon slices.

*4 servings*

## CAPE COD POTATO SALAD

2 cups cubed cooked potatoes
½ cup chopped celery
2 tablespoons chopped chives
    or spring onions
½ cup chopped stuffed olives
few grains of cayenne

½ cup French dressing
½ cup mayonnaise
lettuce
1 hard-cooked egg, finely
    chopped

Mix together the potatoes, celery, chives, olives, cayenne and French dressing. Cover and chill for about 1 hour.

Mix in the mayonnaise. Serve on lettuce and sprinkle with chopped egg.

*4 servings*

## POTATO SALAD, OLD-FASHIONED BOILED DRESSING

Before the advent of commercial mayonnaise, boiled dressing was used. It was tricky to make but well worth the trouble.

3 egg yolks
1 teaspoon white pepper
½ tablespoon salt
1 tablespoon white sugar
1 tablespoon dry mustard

6 tablespoons vinegar
1 tablespoon melted butter
8 medium-size potatoes,
    peeled, cooked and sliced
1 cup chopped celery

Beat egg yolks until thick and lemon-colored.

Mix together the seasonings and vinegar. Put in top part of double boiler. Add beaten egg yolks and melted butter. Cook over boiling water until thick and smooth.

Mix with sliced potatoes and celery. Refrigerate until ready to serve.

*6 to 8 servings*

## HOT POTATO SALAD

4 medium-size potatoes,
    peeled, cooked and sliced
1 teaspoon salt
½ teaspoon freshly ground
    pepper
1 tablespoon minced onion

¼ cup chopped celery
1 tablespoon chopped parsley
2 slices of bacon
2 tablespoons tarragon
    vinegar

Preheat oven to 350° F.

Season the potatoes and mix together with the onion, celery and parsley. Fry bacon until crisp; crumble bacon and reserve fat.

Mix together the vinegar and bacon fat. Pour over the potatoes, toss well, and heat in the oven. Sprinkle with crumbled bacon.

*4 servings*                                                             *quick*

## SCALLOPS LOUIS

2 cups bay scallops, cooked
    and cooled
shredded lettuce
½ cup French dressing
½ cup chili sauce

few drops of Worcestershire
    sauce
1 teaspoon salt
few grains of cayenne

Pile the scallops onto a bed of shredded lettuce.

Mix together the remaining ingredients, pour over the scallops, and serve chilled.

*4 servings*                                                             *quick*

## TOMATO ASPIC

1½ cups tomato juice
1 envelope unflavored
  gelatin
½ teaspoon sugar
1 teaspoon lemon juice
1 teaspoon salt

½ teaspoon pepper
½ teaspoon Worcestershire
  sauce
lettuce
mayonnaise

Heat ½ cup of the tomato juice. Stir in the gelatin and sugar until dissolved. Remove from heat.

Stir in the remaining tomato juice, lemon juice, seasonings and Worcestershire. Pour into a 2-cup mold, and chill until firm.

Turn out onto a bed of lettuce, top with mayonnaise, and serve.

*4 servings*

## CRANBERRY TURKEY MOLD

Here is a popular Nantucket summer salad. The recipe is a very versatile one in that cooked shrimps, scallops, lobster or crabmeat (or a combination of seafoods) may be substituted for the turkey. To stretch the dish, chopped hard-cooked egg and/or additional chopped celery may be added.

1 envelope unflavored
  gelatin, dissolved in ¾
  cup warm water
1 cup small pieces of cold
  cooked turkey
½ cup chopped celery

¼ cup chopped pimientos
½ cup ground cranberries
¾ cup mayonnaise
½ teaspoon salt
1 teaspoon paprika
lettuce leaves

Mix together all the ingredients except lettuce. Spoon into a 3½- to 4-cup mold, and chill until firm.

Unmold onto chilled lettuce leaves.

*4 servings*

# GEMS,
# JOHNNY CAKES
# & BREADS

# GEMS AND JOHNNY CAKES

An old Boston cookbook put out by A. H. Hartley Co. Carpets, 95 and 105 Washington St., Boston, has four recipes for doughnuts, one entitled "good doughnuts." Right underneath it is another recipe, and written in pencil next to one simply entitled "doughnuts" is the word "good." The recipe calls for 1 cup of sweet milk, "less" is written in pencil beside that, one cup of sugar, "⅓" in pencil beside it, one egg, piece of butter the size of a walnut, "2" in pencil, "½" large teaspoonful yeast powder, flour enough to roll. Individuality flourished on Nantucket.

Gems were then so called because they were cooked in a Gem Pan, a cast-iron muffin pan with deep cups holding about 8 ounces each. The present-day gem pans are muffin pans holding 1 ounce in each depression. These hot breads were important then to the cooking on an island because it was easy to run out of yeast bread and there would not be bread enough for supper. Sweet breads and cookies were children quieters and dessert, too, for family suppers and teas, as supper was called English fashion in the midnineteenth century, and were always on hand in case of callers. Dinner was in the middle of the day.

Yeast powder (baking powder) is a mixture of cream of tartar and baking soda, and was probably named that when it was first marketed.

## BREAKFAST BANNOCK

This is a spoon bread. Cornmeal is stone-ground on Nantucket. There were once 12 mills on the island, but now only one remains. In a handwritten cookbook under the word "Bannock" there is a notation, "2 cups meal—1 pint milk—pt. water, 3 eggs," as if only to remind the writer of quantities. Mendon Bannock is made with all milk.

| | |
|---|---|
| 2 cups stone-ground cornmeal | 1 teaspoon salt |
| 2 cups milk | 1 tablespoon sugar |
| 2 cups water | 3 eggs |
| | 2 tablespoons butter |

Preheat oven to 350° F.

Put cornmeal into a large saucepan. Boil milk and water. Pour slowly into cornmeal, stirring to prevent lumps. Cook over low heat until thick. Cool until blood warm. Add salt and sugar. Beat in eggs.

Heat butter in a baking dish in the oven until butter is hot. Pour in Bannock. Bake for 40 minutes, or until brown.

This batter can also be cooked for pancakes on a well-greased griddle.

*4 to 6 servings*

## MENDON BANNOCK

| | |
|---|---|
| 4 cups milk | 1 teaspoon salt |
| 1 cup stone-ground cornmeal | 1 tablespoon sugar |
| 5 eggs, well beaten | 3 tablespoons butter |

Preheat oven to 375° F.

Put milk in the top part of a double boiler and let it get very hot. Pour it gradually over the cornmeal, stirring out lumps.

Return to stove and cook over low heat until thick, stirring all the while. Cool until blood warm. Add eggs, salt and sugar.

Put butter in a baking dish and heat in the oven until hot. Pour in bannock, and bake for 40 minutes, or until brown. Serve immediately.

*6 to 8 servings*

## BLUEBERRY GRIDDLE CAKES

1½ cups milk
1 cup flour
1 teaspoon salt

2 eggs, beaten
1 cup blueberries, washed
bacon fat

Put all ingredients except bacon fat into a bowl. Beat briskly.

Heat griddle, brush with fat, and pour batter with soup ladle onto griddle. Cook cakes until covered with bubbles. Turn, and cook for 3 minutes, until cooked on other side. Serve 4 to 6 to a serving.

*30 pancakes, 3-inch size*                                                    *quick*

## OLD-FASHIONED BUCKWHEAT CAKES

In days gone by ordinary buckwheat cakes were made with buckwheat flour mixed with water and ½ cup "homemade yeast," or starter. They were let stand overnight, then a little salt and baking soda were added, but first a part was saved for the next day's raising. You can still find Nantucket families enjoying the old yeast cakes.

½ cup stone-ground
   cornmeal
2 cups boiling water
½ teaspoon salt
½ cup white flour
1 cup buckwheat flour

½ package dry yeast, or ⅓
   yeast cake, dissolved in ¼
   cup water
¼ teaspoon baking soda,
   dissolved in 2
   tablespoons water

Put cornmeal in a heatproof bowl and pour boiling water over it. Add salt. Let cool.

When lukewarm add white flour and buckwheat flour and dissolved yeast. Beat well. Cover with cloth. Let stand overnight. (Reserve 1 cup if a "starter" is desired.)

In the morning add baking soda. Bake on a hot greased griddle until bubbles cover top; turn, and brown on the other side. Serve with butter and maple syrup.

*4 to 6 servings*

## WAFFLES

| | |
|---|---|
| 2 cups flour | 2 eggs, separated |
| 2 teaspoons baking powder | 1 tablespoon melted |
| ¾ teaspoon salt |    shortening |
| 1¾ cups milk | |

Sift the dry ingredients together.

Add the milk to the egg yolks and stir into the dry ingredients. Add the shortening.

Beat the egg whites until stiff and fold into the batter.

Bake on a well-greased hot waffle iron until brown. Turn once. Serve with butter and syrup.

*4 to 6 servings*                                                                                 *quick*

## BOSTON BROWN BREAD

| | |
|---|---|
| 1 cup whole-wheat or rye | 1 teaspoon salt |
|    flour | 1 teaspoon baking soda |
| 1 cup white flour | ⅔ cup molasses |
| 2 cups cornmeal | ⅔ cup water |

Mix all the ingredients together to make a thin batter.

Pour into a buttered 1½-quart pudding mold with a tight cover, or 3 greased 1-pound coffee tins. Fill two-thirds full.

Set in a pan of boiling water with water halfway up around mold. Keep water boiling. Cover tightly and steam bread for 3 to 4 hours. Add more water as necessary to keep water level even.

*16 servings*

# PORTUGUESE BREAD

This bread should be eaten within 24 hours because there are no preservatives in it.

1½ cups warm water
2 tablespoons brewer's yeast, available in health food stores, or 2 packages dry yeast, dissolved in ½ cup water

2 teaspoons salt
5½ to 6 cups sifted flour
2 tablespoons lard

Mix water, yeast and salt.

Add half the flour; stir well. Add remaining flour; mix well. Put on floured board.

Knead by folding forward and pressing with heel of hands. Turn, press, continue kneading from 10 to 20 minutes until dough is smooth and satiny; the more kneading the better.

Rub a bowl with lard and put dough in it. Turn dough over so that lard is on both top and bottom of dough. Let rise in an unlit oven with a pilot light with door open. Let rise for about 2 hours, or until doubled in bulk. Remove from oven and punch down.

Knead again for 4 or 5 minutes. Let rest for 10 minutes. Form into 2 round loaves on a greased cookie sheet. Let rise until doubled.

Preheat oven to 375° F.

Bake for 35 to 40 minutes, until bread gives off a hollow sound when tapped with a finger. Let cool on rack.

*2 round loaves*

*"Mrs. Grant went to sea with her husband Captain Grant. Once she went ashore at Pitcairn Island to nurse the wife of another captain through a long illness, she complained only of the lack of good white bread."* Nantucket, the Far-Away Island, *William Oliver Stevens*

# PORTUGUESE SWEET BREAD

3 cups milk
½ pound butter
3 packages dry yeast, or 2
   ounces brewer's yeast
4 cups sugar

1½ tablespoons salt
10 eggs, at room temperature
5 to 6 cups flour
2 tablespoons lemon juice
beaten egg for topping

Heat milk. Put butter in a bowl. Pour 1 cup hot milk over butter to melt it.

Put yeast and ½ cup sugar in a small bowl and pour ½ cup hot milk over it. Set aside to prove.

Put remaining sugar in a large mixing bowl, and add the salt and eggs. Mix with both hands, making a rotary motion to beat.

Add all the flour and continue mixing with both hands. Make a well in center and add some of the remaining milk. Mix and knead.

Fold the dough from outside into the center, working dough constantly, punching it down, and adding warm milk and melted butter, then the lemon juice and lastly the yeast mixture. Knead for about 30 minutes in all.

Sprinkle dough with flour. Cover the bowl with wax paper and a blanket. Let rise until doubled in bulk, 4 to 9 hours, depending on room temperature.

Punch down dough and fold toward center. Divide into 6 round loaves and place each in a loaf pan. Dough should half-fill pans. Cover and let rise until it doubles again, 4 to 9 hours.

Preheat oven to 300° F.

Brush loaves with beaten egg and bake for 45 minutes. Remove bread from oven and remove bread from pans. Cool.

*6 loaves*

## YEAST POWDER BREAD

2 cups flour
1 tablespoon yeast (baking)
    powder with cream of
    tartar

½ teaspoon salt
2 tablespoons shortening
    (butter or lard)
1 cup water or milk

Sift flour, baking powder and salt. Cut in shortening. Moisten dough with water or milk.

Knead for 1 minute. Put in a 9-inch-square pan.

Bake for 15 to 20 minutes. Cut into squares.

*4 to 6 servings*                                              *quick*

## BUTTERMILK BISCUITS

4 cups flour
2 teaspoons salt
½ teaspoon baking soda

6 tablespoons lard
2 cups buttermilk

Preheat oven to 425° F.

Sift flour, salt and baking soda. Cut in the lard, and add the buttermilk, making a relatively stiff dough.

Knead slightly. Roll out on a floured board to ½-inch thickness, and cut into biscuits.

Place on a greased baking sheet and bake for 10 to 12 minutes.

*4 servings*                                                  *quick*

## SKILLET BISCUITS

2 tablespoons lard
2 cups flour
2 teaspoons baking powder

1 teaspoon salt
1 cup milk or water
bacon fat

Cut lard into flour that has been sifted with baking powder and salt until mixture has the texture of cornmeal.

Add milk or water to make a soft dough. Cut into wedges.

Brush an iron skillet with bacon fat, and fry the wedges on each side over medium-low heat until brown. Turn heat to low and cover pot. Cook until centers are done, about 15 minutes more.

*6 servings*                                                                                   *quick*

## DUMPLINGS

These dumplings are like a steamed biscuit. They can be steamed separately or on top of a stew.

| | |
|---|---|
| 3 cups flour | ¼ cup lard |
| 1 teaspoon salt | 1 cup milk, approximately |
| 2 teaspoons baking powder | |

Sift flour, salt and baking powder together. Mix lard with flour mixture until it is like cornmeal. Add enough of the milk to moisten the mixture, but don't make the dough too wet to roll out.

Roll out and cut into small rounds or squares. Steam in a single layer on a rack in a tightly covered saucepan for 20 minutes. Or do not roll out, but drop by spoonfuls onto boiling stew, cover the pot, and steam for 20 minutes without opening the cover.

*8 servings*                                                                                   *quick*

VARIATION: These can be used to make a dessert like a cobbler with stewed cranberries. Cook 2 cups cranberries with 2 cups sugar until the sauce is quite thick. Strain while hot and spoon over steamed dumplings to serve.

## SHEARING BUNS

Sheepshearing, a big festival like a county fair in Nantucket in the eighteenth century, was always held on the second and third days nearest the twentieth of the sixth month. All kinds of foods were served and sold at this festival. *Nantucket the Far-Away Island,* William Oliver Stevens

2 cups milk
¼ pound butter
3½ cups flour, sifted
1½ tablespoons brewer's
    yeast, or 1 package dry
    yeast

¼ teaspoon salt
2 eggs, beaten
1½ cups plus 2 tablespoons
    sugar
¼ cup dried currants
1 extra egg white, beaten

Boil milk. Add butter. When cool, add ½ cup flour to make a thin batter, and the yeast and salt. Let rise overnight.

In the morning add the beaten whole eggs and work them in. Repeat with 1½ cups sugar and the currants. Add remaining flour gradually until the dough is stiff enough to mold, though not as stiff as biscuit dough.

Let rise again until dough is doubled in bulk, 4 to 5 hours. Form dough into cakes. Lay them close together in a pan, and let rise again until doubled.

Preheat oven to 350° F.

Bake buns until they are a good, light brown. Brush the buns with the egg white beaten with remaining 2 tablespoons sugar.

*45 buns*

---

## GOOD DOUGHNUTS

1 cup, less 1 tablespoon,
    sweet milk
⅓ cup sugar
1 egg

3 tablespoons butter
1 teaspoon baking powder
2½ to 3 cups flour
1 pound lard for deep-frying

Mix milk, sugar, egg and butter. Sift baking powder with flour. Add to milk mixture and mix well.

Roll out on a floured cloth, and cut with a doughnut cutter; or use a biscuit cutter, and cut holes with a sharp knife.

Heat lard in skillet until barely smoking (360° F.). Cook doughnuts in hot lard until brown on one side; turn and brown on other side.

Drain on paper towels or brown paper bag. Serve plain or sprinkled with powdered sugar and cinnamon.

*12 doughnuts*                                                        *quick*

# NANTUCKET WONDERS

A recipe for Wonders recently appeared in a cookbook published by the United Nations. The recipe was attributed to Dahomey. Perhaps a Dahomeyan sailed on a Nantucket Whaling Ship years ago, or perhaps a whaling captain entertained a tribal leader aboard ship who liked the dessert. But wherever they are found, Wonders are strictly Nantucket, and crunchier and tastier than doughnuts because of the way they are cut and scored.

7 tablespoons melted butter
3 eggs, slightly beaten
¼ teaspoon baking soda
    dissolved in 1 tablespoon
    boiling water

6 tablespoons sugar
½ tablespoon grated nutmeg
½ teaspoon salt
2½ cups flour
lard for deep-frying

Mix everything except lard into a dough.

Flour a board and roll out the dough, a couple of spoonfuls at a time, until about ¼ inch thick. Cut into strips 2 inches wide and 3 inches long, or other shapes. Score with a jagger wheel lengthwise and crosswise.

Fry in deep fat heated to 365° F., a few at a time, until brown. Drain on paper napkins.

*18 Wonders*                                                            *quick*

---

# BLUEBERRY MUFFINS

3 cups flour
1 tablespoon baking powder
4 tablespoons sugar
½ teaspoon salt
1 cup milk

1 egg
5 tablespoons melted butter
1 cup blueberries mixed with
    2 tablespoons sugar

Preheat oven to 400° F.

Mix and sift the flour, baking powder, sugar and salt. Beat together the milk and egg, and mix with the dry ingredients. Stir in the butter and blueberries.

Drop into buttered muffin tins, and bake for 15 to 20 minutes.

*36 muffins*                                                            *quick*

## CRANBERRY MUFFINS

1 egg, lightly beaten
1 orange, juice and grated rind
⅔ cup milk or water
½ cup melted butter
2 cups flour
¾ teaspoon salt

2 teaspoons baking powder
½ cup sugar
1 cup cranberries, cut into
    halves, or whole
    blueberries
½ cup nuts, chopped

Preheat oven to 400° F.

Mix together the egg, orange juice and rind, milk and butter. Mix together the flour, salt, baking powder and sugar.

Beat the dry mixture into the egg-milk mixture. Mixture need not be smooth; it can be lumpy. Stir in the cranberries and nuts.

Grease a 12-cup muffin pan and fill the cups three-quarters full. Bake for 20 to 25 minutes, or until golden. This batter can be baked in gem pans or a ring mold or loaf pan, if you prefer.

*24 muffins*                                                      *quick*

---

## GRAHAM GEMS

1 cup graham (whole-wheat) flour
1 cup all-purpose flour
1 teaspoon baking powder

1 cup milk
1 tablespoon molasses
1 tablespoon butter

Preheat oven to 375° F.

Mix whole-wheat flour, all-purpose flour and baking powder. Mix milk, molasses and butter. Combine the mixtures.

Butter a gem pan; fill two-thirds full with mixture. Bake for 15 to 20 minutes.

*6 gems if baked in old iron gem pans*
*40 gems if baked in modern 1-ounce gem pans*                     *quick*

---

## OLD-FASHIONED JOHNNY CAKE

1 cup stone-ground cornmeal
½ teaspoon salt

2 cups milk or water

Preheat oven to 350° F.

Mix cornmeal and salt. Heat milk or water until just boiling. Pour slowly over cornmeal. Stir out lumps.

Pour onto greased baking pan. Batter should be ¼ inch thick. Bake for 25 to 30 minutes, until crisp. Split and spread with butter.

*4 to 6 servings*                                                *quick*

## NANTUCKET JOHNNY CAKE

butter
2 cups stone-ground
    cornmeal (Indian meal)
1 cup flour

1 tablespoon baking powder
2 cups milk
⅓ cup molasses

Preheat oven to 375° F.

Butter a 1½-quart baking pan.

Mix meal, flour, baking powder, milk and molasses together, and pour into pan. Bake for 30 to 40 minutes.

*6 servings*                                                *quick*

## JOHNNY GEMS

1 cup sour milk
⅓ cup melted lard
½ cup molasses
1 egg

⅛ teaspoon salt
1 teaspoon baking soda
1 cup cornmeal (Indian meal)
2 cups flour

Preheat oven to 350° F.

Butter a cast-iron gem pan and put in oven. Put all ingredients in a large bowl and beat until mixed.

Divide the mixture evenly into the cups of an iron gem pan, or put 1 tablespoon per cup in 1-ounce gem pans. Put in oven.

Increase heat to 400° F. and finish baking, about 15 or 20 minutes.

*12 gems if baked in old iron gem pans*
*80 gems if baked in modern 1-ounce gem pans*                *quick*

# INDIAN PUFFS

Stone- or water-ground cornmeal was always called Indian meal in the early days of the country.

| | |
|---|---|
| 2 cups milk | 1 tablespoon sugar |
| 4 tablespoons stone-ground cornmeal | 1 teaspoon salt |
| | 3 eggs, well beaten |

Preheat oven to 375° F.

Put milk in top part of a double boiler and set over boiling water. When scalding hot pour it gradually into the cornmeal, stirring all the while. Add sugar and salt. Return mixture to top of double boiler and cook over boiling water for 5 minutes.

Remove top pan from boiling water and let the mixture cool until blood warm. Add the well-beaten eggs.

Butter 8 custard cups. Fill half full with mixture. Bake for 20 to 25 minutes.

*4 servings, 8 puffs*                                                          *quick*

---

# POP UPS

| | |
|---|---|
| 2 unbeaten eggs | 1 cup flour |
| 1 cup milk | ½ teaspoon salt |

Break eggs into a bowl; add milk, flour and salt. Mix well with flour, ignoring lumps.

Fill cold greased muffin tins three-quarters full. Put in cold oven. Turn oven to 450° F. and bake for 30 minutes. Do not open the oven during the baking time.

*12 pop ups*                                                                  *quick*

# CAKES
# & COOKIES

## SPICED MOLASSES COFFEE CAKE

¼ pound butter
1 cup sugar
2 eggs, beaten
1 cup molasses
2½ cups flour
1 teaspoon each of ground
    cloves, cinnamon and
    allspice

½ cup raisins
2 tablespoons chopped citron
1 teaspoon baking soda
    dissolved in ½ cup
    prepared coffee

Preheat oven to 350° F.

Cream butter and beat in the sugar, beaten eggs and molasses.

Sift flour and spices together. Roll raisins and citron in flour and set aside. Add flour to butter mixture gradually, beating all the while.

Add baking soda and coffee, then raisins and citron. Pour into a greased 1½-quart baking pan. Bake for 35 to 40 minutes.

*8 servings*

## BLUEBERRY PANDOWDY

1 quart blueberries
1 cup sugar
½ teaspoon ground ginger

3 tablespoons butter
1 recipe Skillet Biscuits
   (p. 138)

Preheat oven to 350° F.

Butter a baking dish or pie pan. Wash and pick over blueberries. Put in pie pan. Sprinkle with sugar and ginger. Dot with butter.

Make biscuits; roll or pat out. Cover blueberries with biscuit dough. Bake for 30 minutes, or until biscuits are light brown.

*6 to 8 servings*                                              *quick*

## CUPCAKES

½ pound butter, softened
3 cups sugar
4 eggs
4½ cups flour
½ teaspoon baking soda

1 teaspoon grated nutmeg
1 teaspoon each of ground
   ginger and cinnamon
3 cups raisins
1 cup milk

Cream butter until lemon-colored. Add sugar and beat until fluffy. Add eggs, one at a time. Sift flour, baking soda and spices together.

Preheat oven to 350° F.

Put raisins in water to cover and bring to a boil. Drain, and roll in flour.

Add flour mixture alternately with milk to butter mixture. Add raisins.

Butter cupcake tins; fill two-thirds full with batter. Bake for 15 to 20 minutes.

*About 4 dozen cupcakes*

NOTE: Puffed raisins treated with vegetable oil do not need to be boiled for this recipe or for any of the others using raisins.

# QUICK BOSTON CREAM PIE

CAKE

| | |
|---|---|
| 2 eggs | 2 teaspoons baking powder |
| ½ cup granulated sugar | ¼ cup milk |
| ¾ cup flour | confectioners' sugar |

Preheat oven to 350° F.

Beat eggs and granulated sugar until fluffy. Sift flour and baking powder together, and add alternately to the egg mixture with the milk.

Bake in a single buttered cake tin for 30 to 35 minutes. Cool for 10 minutes. Turn out.

CUSTARD

| | |
|---|---|
| ½ cup sugar | 1 tablespoon flour |
| 1 egg | 1 cup milk, boiling |

Beat sugar and egg together; add flour.

Bring milk to a boil, reduce heat, and stir milk slowly into the sugar-egg mixture. Stir until thick.

When cake is cold, split into halves horizontally. Spread custard between halves. Dust with confectioners' sugar. Cut as one would a pie.

*6 servings*

# FARMER'S CAKE

| | |
|---|---|
| 1 cup molasses | 2 teaspoons ground |
| ½ cup sour milk | cinnamon |
| ⅓ cup butter | 1 teaspoon ground cloves |
| 1 cup sugar | 1 cup dried apples, soaked |
| 1 egg, lightly beaten | overnight and chopped, |
| 2 cups flour | or 2 cups chopped fresh |
| 1 teaspoon baking soda | apples |

Preheat oven to 375° F.

Simmer molasses for 2 hours. Cool, and stir in the sour milk.

Cream butter, add sugar, and beat until light. Stir in the egg. Sift flour, baking soda and spices together.

Add the molasses mixture and flour mixture alternately to butter mixture. Add apples.

Pour into a buttered 2-quart baking pan. Bake for 40 minutes, or until the cake springs back when touched.

*16 servings*

---

# FRUITCAKE

½ pound butter, softened
2¼ cups sugar
4 eggs, separated
¼ teaspoon baking soda
1 cup milk
1 cup raisins
1 cup dried currants

¼ cup sliced citron
3 cups flour
1 teaspoon grated nutmeg
1 teaspoon each of ground
    cinnamon, cloves and
    allspice

Preheat oven to 300° F.

Cream butter, gradually add sugar and beat until fluffy. Add well-beaten egg yolks. Dissolve baking soda in milk.

Roll raisins, currants and citron in flour. Sift remaining flour with spices. Add flour and milk alternately to the butter mixture. Fold in fruits.

Beat egg whites until stiff. Fold in.

Spoon into a 3-quart ring mold or 2 loaf pans, 9 by 5 by 3 inches, well buttered and lined with buttered paper. Bake for 1½ hours.

## HARD SUGAR GINGERBREAD

5 cups flour
3 cups sugar
1½ teaspoons baking soda
2 tablespoons ground ginger

1 pound butter, softened
3 eggs
1½ cups milk

Preheat oven to 375° F.

Sift together flour, sugar, baking soda and ginger. Work in butter until the mixture is as fine as cornmeal.

Mix together the eggs and milk, and add to flour mixture. Work the liquids in well.

Roll out very thin, and place on a large baking sheet. Bake until brown, 5 to 10 minutes.

"Will keep good for months."

## SOFT GINGERBREAD

2 cups flour
1 teaspoon ground ginger
⅔ cup sour milk
½ cup molasses
1 teaspoon baking soda
    dissolved in 2
    tablespoons boiling water

2 tablespoons butter
½ cup sugar

Preheat oven to 325° F.

Sift together the flour and ginger. Mix sour milk, molasses and baking soda.

Cream butter, add sugar, and mix in the flour and milk mixtures alternately.

Butter a 1½-quart baking pan. Spread batter in pan, and bake for 35 to 45 minutes. Serve hot with butter or cream.

*8 to 10 servings*

## MINCEMEAT SHORTCAKE

This recipe can be used for any shortcake, with fresh or dried fruits or berries.

| | |
|---|---|
| 4 cups flour | 2 cups milk |
| 1 tablespoon baking powder | 1 egg, beaten |
| 1 tablespoon sugar | 1 quart mincemeat |
| ¼ pound butter | 1 cup heavy cream, whipped |

Preheat oven to 375° F.

Sift flour, baking powder and sugar together. Cut butter into it, or blend it into flour with fingers until mixture is fine.

Add milk and egg, and form into a ball of dough. Divide into 2 portions.

Roll each ball of dough into a round about 1 inch thick. Bake the rounds in 2 round pans.

When done, split the cakes in two. Lightly butter lower half of each and put a layer of mincemeat on it. Add a layer of whipped cream. Lay on the top crust and serve while hot.

*10 to 12 servings*

## MOLASSES BLUEBERRY CAKE

| | |
|---|---|
| 2 eggs, lightly beaten | 1 teaspoon baking soda |
| ½ cup molasses | 1 teaspoon each of ground |
| ½ cup melted lard | cinnamon and allspice |
| 1 cup sour milk | 1 teaspoon grated nutmeg |
| 1½ cups sugar | 2½ cups blueberries, washed, |
| 2 cups flour | drained and floured |
| 1 teaspoon salt | |

Preheat oven to 350° F.

Mix together the eggs, molasses, lard and sour milk. Mix together the sugar, flour, salt, baking soda and spices.

Beat the egg mixture into the dry mixture, using a wire whisk or electric mixer. Stir in the floured blueberries.

Spoon into a greased 10-inch tube pan. Bake for about 30 minutes, or until a straw inserted in center comes out clean.

*24 servings*

# ONE, TWO, THREE, FOUR CAKE

Easy to remember without a cookbook.

| | |
|---|---|
| 1 cup (½ pound) butter, softened | 3 cups flour |
| 2 cups sugar | 1 cup milk |
| 4 eggs | 1 teaspoon vanilla extract |

Preheat oven to 350° F.

Cream butter, add sugar, and beat until fluffy. Add eggs; beat well. Add flour alternately with the milk. Add vanilla.

Spoon into 3 layer-cake pans lined with buttered brown paper. Bake for 35 to 40 minutes, or until cake springs back when touched.

Cool on a rack for 10 minutes. Remove pans.

CHOCOLATE FILLING

| | |
|---|---|
| ½ cup grated unsweetened chocolate | 1 egg yolk |
| ½ cup milk | 1 cup sugar |
| | 1 teaspoon vanilla extract |

Cook all together over low heat until the mixture is stiff. Cool, and spread between layers.

FROSTING FOR CAKE

| | |
|---|---|
| 1 egg white | 1½ cups confectioners' sugar |

Beat egg white until stiff. Gradually add the sugar. When frosting is stiff, spread over cake. Set aside until ready to serve.

*"You can tell when a cake is done, it sings."*

## QUARTER PECK, OLD-FASHIONED WEDDING CAKE

This recipe is adapted from one belonging to Mrs. Peter Foulger, A.D. 1674, which required 40 eggs! It was "put to bed overnight between warm cushions," to rise, and was cooked the following day.

| | |
|---|---|
| 1 cup (½ pound) butter, softened | 2 packages dry yeast, or 2 tablespoons brewer's |
| 1 cup sugar | yeast, or 1 cup |
| 1 cup milk | homemade yeast (starter) |
| 5 cups flour | |

Cream butter and add sugar gradually. Add milk, flour and yeast. Beat all together and let rise overnight.

| | |
|---|---|
| 1 cup (½ pound) butter, softened | 1½ tablespoons grated nutmeg |
| 1 cup sugar | 1½ tablespoons grated mace |
| 1 cup white wine | 5 eggs, slightly beaten |
| 3 cups raisins, washed and boiled | |

The next morning, mix the remaining ingredients into the dough thoroughly. Form into loaves, and put into 6 well-buttered loaf pans, 9 by 5 by 3 inches. Let dough rise again until doubled in bulk.

Preheat oven to 350° F.

Bake for 45 minutes to 1 hour.

## MRS. W'S GINGERSNAPS

From an Old Nantucket cookbook, "Mix hard, roll thin," are the instructions with these cookies. Bake in a very quick oven.

1 cup molasses, heated
¼ pound butter
½ cup sugar
1 teaspoon ground ginger

1 teaspoon baking soda
2½ to 3 cups flour, or
    enough to roll out

Preheat oven to 400° F.

Mix molasses, butter and sugar. Sift ginger, baking soda and 2½ cups flour. Combine the two mixtures to make a stiff dough. Add more flour if necessary.

Roll out thin, and cut into 1½-inch cookies. Put on a greased cookie sheet. Bake for 5 to 7 minutes.

Let cool. Store in can or cookie jar away from humidity.

*about 3 dozen snaps*

## JUMBLES

We found 3 recipes for Jumbles in the old cookbooks, each so different from the other that they should have different names. This was the best.

4 tablespoons butter, softened
⅓ cup granulated sugar
1 tablespoon brandy or sour
    cream

1¾ cups flour
1½ teaspoons baking powder
1 egg, beaten
confectioners' sugar

Preheat oven to 375° F.

Cream butter, add granulated sugar, and beat until fluffy. Add brandy. Sift flour and baking powder into butter mixture. Mix well.

Roll out on floured board or cloth. Cut into long narrow strips. Press lightly to make strips round. Roll in beaten egg, then in confectioners' sugar. Wind each strip round and round to form small cakes.

Bake for 10 to 12 minutes.

*12 jumbles* *quick*

## MOLASSES COOKIES

2 teaspoons baking soda
1 cup molasses
2½ cups flour
½ teaspoon salt

1 teaspoon ground ginger
⅜ pound butter or lard
½ cup water

Preheat oven to 375° F.

Dissolve baking soda in molasses. Sift flour with salt and ginger.

Cut butter or lard into flour mixture until it is as fine as cornmeal. Mix with molasses and water. If it is too soft to roll, add enough flour to make it stiff enough. Chill.

Cut into cookies. Put on greased cookie sheet. Bake for 12 to 15 minutes.

*2 dozen cookies*

*"There was always a deep sugar scraping at the bottom of the molasses barrel, part was used for pancake syrup and the rest was used for taffy."*
*Louise Gibson, Nantucket*

## SINFUL COOKIES

An Orange Street chef makes these cookies each year to give away to his neighbors for Christmas. They are the first present opened on Orange Street.

1 pound unsalted butter
1 cup granulated sugar
2 cups almonds in their skins, finely ground

3 cups pastry or all-purpose flour
2 vanilla beans
1 pound confectioners' sugar

Preheat oven to 325° F.

Cream the butter, add granulated sugar, and beat. Add the almonds and the flour gradually.

Drop by teaspoons onto an ungreased cookie sheet. Bake for 15 to 20 minutes.

Grate the seeds of the vanilla beans into the confectioners' sugar. While the cookies are still warm dip them into the vanilla sugar mixture.

*20 small cookies*                                                    *quick*

---

## CRANBERRY OATMEAL COOKIES

2 cups flour
2 cups sugar
4 teaspoons baking powder
1 teaspoon salt
1 teaspoon grated nutmeg
1 cup vegetable shortening

2 eggs
1 orange, juice and grated rind
3 cups rolled oats
1 cup cranberries, cut into halves

Preheat oven to 375° F.

Sift flour, sugar, baking powder, salt and nutmeg together.

Add shortening, eggs, orange juice and rind. Mix well. Stir in oats and cranberries.

Drop by tablespoons onto greased cookie sheets, and bake for 10 to 12 minutes.

Remove from oven. Cool for 10 minutes.

*4 dozen cookies*                                                    *quick*

# PUDDINGS
# & PIES

# PUDDINGS

Puddings were important in the days when Nantucket was isolated from the mainland a good many days of the year. Made from staple foods such as flour, sugar, salt, eggs, spices, dried fruits, they didn't depend on the seasons.

Boiled puddings were popular for this reason and for another equally important: Ovens were often unpredictable with wood and coal fires, either too hot or too cold. A boiling pot was more reliable; water had to be added from time to time when boiling a pudding, but there was time to prepare other things while it was cooking. Also it was possible to read or take a dip in the sea.

*Nantucket Receipts,* compiled in 1874 by Mrs. Susan Hosmer, added to by Miss Caroline Tallant, and then by Mrs. Maria L. Owen, and later, in 1915, edited by Harry D. Turner, applies these rules to boiled puddings.

"Puddings which are to be boiled should be put in boiling water and the water kept boiling. Stout white jean or cotton drilling, make a good pudding cloth (30 x 30 inches unbleached muslin or old sailcloth). It should be large enough

158

to allow the ends to hang out of the pot after the pudding is put in. Then put on the cover and keep it steady. This is necessary in a berry pudding to prevent the cracking of the crust. Wet the cloth in hot or cold water before flouring it for the pudding."

An easy way to boil a pudding is to put the floured cloth in a heatproof bowl, add the pudding mixture, and close tightly, leaving space for the pudding (two-thirds full) to rise. Set the bowl on a trivet in a pot of boiling water that reaches halfway up the side of the bowl.

A pudding can also be cooked in a mold with a tight cover, well buttered inside including the cover. The mold is then set on a trivet in boiling water halfway up the side, enough to keep up a good steam. The pot should be covered, of course.

Boiled puddings and well-baked puddings are usually served with a sauce: brandy, lemon, nutmeg, hard or berry sauce.

Here are several recipes for boiled and baked puddings; also a boiled Indian Pudding which was served with butter.

## AMHERST PUDDING

3 cups flour
1 teaspoon salt
1 teaspoon baking soda
1 teaspoon grated nutmeg
½ teaspoon ground ginger

1 cup very finely chopped suet
1 cup milk
1 cup molasses
2 cups raisins

Sift flour, salt, baking soda and spices together. Mix in suet; add milk and molasses. Roll raisins in flour and add.

Flour a pudding cloth (see above), or butter a pudding mold. Fill with the batter.

Boil or steam in pudding mold for 3 hours. To unmold, dip into cold water for a few seconds, place a plate over mold, and turn right side up.

*12 servings*

## BOILED BERRY PUDDING, NUTMEG SAUCE

4 cups flour
1 cup (½ pound) butter
¾ cup water, approximately

4 cups berries, picked over
   and washed

Cut butter into flour until fine. Add enough of the water to make a dough that forms a ball. Roll out this dough on a floured cloth. Lift it carefully with the cloth and lay it in a heatproof bowl.

Pour in the berries. Close the dough over the berries.

Tie the ends of the cloth tight and set the bowl on a trivet in boiling water. Boil for 2 hours. Serve with Nutmeg Sauce.

*8 servings*

NUTMEG SAUCE

2 cups sugar
⅔ cup water

1 tablespoon vinegar
1 teaspoon grated nutmeg

Put sugar, water and vinegar in a saucepan, and bring to a rolling boil. Add nutmeg. Serve hot or cold.

*about 2½ cups*                                              *quick*

## COLD BERRY PUDDING

18 slices of bread
butter, softened
4 cups raspberries, picked
   over and washed

2 cups powdered sugar

Remove crusts from bread, and butter the slices.

Line a 2-quart glass dish with 6 slices of bread, buttered side up. Cover with half of the berries, and sprinkle with 1 cup powdered sugar. Cover these with 6 slices of buttered bread, remaining half of the berries and sugar. Cover with remaining 6 slices of bread, buttered side down.

Cover with a plate, and put a weight on the plate. Refrigerate for 24 hours before serving.

*8 servings*

## STEWED BLACKBERRIES

1 quart blackberries                    1 tablespoon flour
¼ cup sugar

Wash and pick over blackberries, and put in a saucepan with just the water that clings to them. Simmer over low heat.

As they stew add sugar and flour mixed together. Add more sugar if berries are very tart. Cook until thick.

Eat with milk or crackers and milk. Also good with vanilla ice cream. This is an excellent summer dessert.

*4 to 6 servings*                                                    *quick*

---

## VERY SPECIAL BREAD AND BUTTER PUDDING

8 slices of stale bread, ½ inch       ½ cup sugar
    thick                             3 eggs, beaten
6 tablespoons butter, softened        ¼ teaspoon salt
¼ teaspoon ground                     4 cups milk
    cinnamon or grated
    nutmeg

Remove crusts from bread and spread slices with butter. Butter a loaf pan, 9 by 5 by 3 inches, or baking dish and put bread slices in, buttered side down.

Mix cinnamon into sugar; add to eggs. Add salt and milk and pour over bread. Let stand to absorb milk for 20 to 30 minutes.

Preheat oven to 325° F.

Bake for 1 hour. Serve with maple syrup.

*6 to 8 servings*

# BROWN BETTY WITH HARD SAUCE

Brown Betty is made with brown sugar, but we have never heard of a White Betty.

6 medium-size apples, pared and cored
1 cup brown sugar
1 teaspoon ground cinnamon
1 teaspoon grated nutmeg

2 tablespoons butter or very finely chopped beef suet
1 cup cracker or bread crumbs
1 cup cold water

Preheat oven to 375° F.

Chop apples fine. Butter a baking dish. Spread a layer of apples on the bottom, and sprinkle with brown sugar mixed with spices and 1 tablespoon butter cut into pieces. Cover with a thin layer of crumbs.

Repeat procedure with remaining ingredients. Pour water over.

Bake for 30 minutes, or until brown. If desired, omit the butter and sugar, and serve hot with hard sauce.

*8 servings*                                                                *quick*

HARD SAUCE

½ pound butter, softened
3 cups confectioners' sugar

2 teaspoons vanilla extract or grated nutmeg or bourbon whiskey

Cream butter; add sugar gradually, beating all the time until sauce is creamy.

Add flavoring. Put in serving dish and refrigerate until ready to use.

*about 2 cups sauce*                                                        *quick*

---

# CABINET PUDDING

sponge cake, or other stale cake
4 maraschino cherries
butter
4 egg yolks

1 tablespoon sugar
½ cup milk
¼ teaspoon vanilla extract
2 egg whites, beaten stiff

Cut stale cake into narrow strips. Cut cherries into halves.

Butter a pudding mold and arrange cherries on the bottom in a pattern. Line sides of mold with cake strips. If there are pieces of icing, break them into small pieces and put them in the mold.

Beat egg yolks; add the sugar, milk and vanilla. Stir until sugar is dissolved. Fold in egg whites. Pour the custard slowly into the mold. Cover mold with buttered brown paper, or its own cover.

Steam on a trivet with boiling water halfway up the side of the mold. Simmer for 1 hour, adding more boiling water if necessary. Unmold by dipping mold into cold water briefly.

*6 servings*

---

## STEAMED CHOCOLATE PUDDING

4 tablespoons butter, softened
¾ cup sugar
2 eggs
2½ cups flour
4 teaspoons baking powder
¼ teaspoon salt

1 cup milk
3 ounces (3 squares) unsweetened chocolate, melted
whipped cream

Cream butter, add sugar, and beat until frothy; add eggs.

Sift flour, baking powder and salt, and add alternately with milk. Add melted chocolate.

Pour into a well-buttered mold two-thirds full, or a well-floured pudding cloth. Cover mold tightly or tie cloth.

Set on a trivet in pan of boiling water halfway up the side of the mold. Boil for 1½ hours. Add more boiling water if necessary to keep water at proper level.

To unmold dip into cold water and turn onto a serving dish. To reheat, steam over hot water. Serve with whipped cream or ice cream.

*12 servings*

# CRANBERRY DUMPLINGS

1½ cups flour
¼ cup lard or vegetable
   shortening
½ teaspoon salt

5 tablespoons water,
   approximately
1½ cups cranberries

Mix flour, lard and salt until mixture is reduced to fine crumbs. Add water to make a soft dough. Roll out, and divide into 4 squares.

Pick over and wash cranberries; dry. Cut each berry into halves. Put a large handful of cranberries on each square of dough. Pinch squares together well at tops.

Drop into a kettle of boiling water, reduce to a simmer, and cook for 45 minutes.

*4 dumplings*

SUGAR SAUCE

2 cups sugar
1 cup water
⅛ teaspoon cream of tartar

1 tablespoon butter
¼ teaspoon grated nutmeg

Cook sugar, water and cream of tartar until syrup thickens. Add butter and nutmeg. Serve over dumplings.

*about 2½ cups*

# CRANBERRY PUDDING

2 cups milk
2 cups cranberries
1 tablespoon baking powder

½ cup sugar
2 cups flour
½ teaspoon salt

Mix all ingredients into a thick batter.

Steam in a floured pudding cloth or buttered mold for 2 hours.

Serve with maple syrup.

*8 servings*

## OLD-FASHIONED BAKED INDIAN PUDDING

4 cups milk
1 cup stone-ground cornmeal
   (Indian meal)

½ cup molasses
butter

Preheat oven to 300° F.

Heat milk to just below boiling; pour it gradually over the corn-meal. Add molasses; mix well.

Pour into a well-buttered baking pan. Bake for 5 to 6 hours.

If desired, the meal and milk can be cooked in a double boiler until thickened, then mixed with molasses and baked for 3 hours. Serve hot or cold.

*12 servings*

---

*"Scalded yellow meal with molasses was served daily, and occasionally salt fish and potatoes, aboard a whaleship."* The Nantucket Scrap Basket

---

## BOILED INDIAN PUDDING

4 cups milk
2 cups stone-ground
   cornmeal (Indian meal)

1 cup molasses
2, 3, 4 or 5 eggs

Bring the milk to a boil and add gradually to the meal, mixing it thoroughly. Stir in the molasses.

Beat the eggs and stir them into the pudding.

Wet and flour a pudding cloth, or grease a mold. Put cloth into a bowl, and pour in pudding. Bring the corners of the cloth together and tie tight with a string about 3 inches above level of pudding. Set on a trivet in boiling water, and keep at a slow boil until done, about 2½ hours.

If in a mold, cover the mold and set on a trivet in water about halfway up the side of the mold, replacing water as it boils down.

*14 to 16 servings*

## PEARS IN SYRUP

2 cups water
1 cup sugar
8 pears, peeled, cored and
   halved, or 1 can (16
   ounces)

2 pieces of whole dried
   gingerroot, cracked
4 strips of lemon rind (zest)

Put water and sugar to boil in a pan large enough so that pear halves will be covered.

When syrup boils add the pear halves, ginger and lemon zest. If canned pears are used, substitute the juice for part of the water. Cook only until pears are tender. Cool.

*4 servings*                                              *quick*

---

## BOILED CHRISTMAS PLUM PUDDING

½ cup finely chopped beef
   suet
¾ cup molasses
2¼ cups flour
¼ teaspoon salt
1 teaspoon baking soda
1 cup milk

2 cups raisins, boiled
1 teaspoon grated nutmeg
1 teaspoon ground cloves
1 tablespoon chopped citron
2 ounces claret
2 ounces brandy

Mix suet and molasses; add flour and salt. Dissolve the baking soda in milk; add to suet mixture.

Flour the raisins and add with spices and citron. Add claret and brandy.

Spoon into a buttered pudding mold filled two-thirds full, or into a well-floured cloth, and set on a trivet in boiling water halfway up the side of mold. Boil for 3 hours.

To unmold plunge mold into cold water for 1 minute, and turn out.

*10 servings*

## QUEEN OF PUDDINGS

2 cups bread crumbs
4 cups milk
1 cup granulated sugar
4 eggs, separated
1 lemon, grated rind and
   juice

2 tablespoons butter
beach plum jelly
½ cup confectioners' sugar

Preheat oven to 350° F.

Mix bread crumbs, milk and granulated sugar. Beat egg yolks and add to bread-crumb mixture; beat.

Grate lemon rind into mixture. Add butter. Mix well and pour into a buttered 2½-quart baking dish.

Bake until knife comes clean. When done spread with slices of jelly.

Beat egg whites to a stiff froth; add confectioners' sugar and lemon juice. Spread this meringue over all. Reduce oven to 250° F. Brown meringue lightly in oven for 15 or 20 minutes.

*8 servings*

## OLD-FASHIONED RICE PUDDING

4 cups milk
½ cup uncooked rice
½ teaspoon salt

¾ cup sugar
⅛ teaspoon grated nutmeg
butter

Preheat oven to 325° F.

Mix milk, rice, salt, sugar and nutmeg. Pour into a well-buttered baking dish.

Bake for 3 hours. Stir pudding 3 times during cooking. (Two eggs can be added the last time pudding is stirred.) Do not stir for last 30 minutes. Serve hot or cold.

*4 to 6 servings*

# PORT-WINE JELLY

This makes a fine company dessert.

2 envelopes unflavored
   gelatin
½ cup cold water
½ cup boiling water
¾ cup sugar

1½ cups port wine
juice of 2 lemons
½ cup rum
1 cup heavy cream, whipped

Put gelatin in a bowl with the cold water to soak.

Add boiling water to gelatin; stir well. Add sugar, wine, lemon juice and rum.

Rub a 4-cup mold with peanut oil. Pour in gelatin mixture. Chill for 3 to 4 hours.

Unmold, and serve on dessert plates with whipped cream.

*6 to 8 servings*

# RAISIN RICE PUDDING

"Five times the quantity of milk to rice. Two cups of rice, 10 cups of milk, 3 eggs." from a handwritten recipe book

1 cup uncooked rice
5 cups milk
2 eggs, beaten

½ cup raisins (optional)
1 teaspoon grated nutmeg

Put rice and milk in top part of a double boiler. Stir in beaten eggs.

Cook over boiling water for 1½ hours.

Add raisins and nutmeg for last 30 minutes of cooking.

*8 to 12 servings*

## SPANISH CREAM

2 cups milk

2 teaspoons unflavored
   gelatin

3 eggs, separated

1 cup sugar

1 teaspoon vanilla extract

Bring milk to a boil; add gelatin. Beat egg yolks and stir into milk. Add sugar.

Cook, stirring, for 10 to 15 minutes, until thick. Add vanilla. Beat egg whites stiff and fold into custard.

Remove from stove and pour into an oiled 4-cup mold. Cool and refrigerate.

*4 to 6 servings*

## BAKED TAPIOCA PUDDING

1 cup tapioca

4 cups milk

1 cup sugar

4 eggs, beaten

1 tablespoon butter

Soak tapioca in milk overnight.

Preheat oven to 375° F.

Add sugar and eggs to tapioca.

Butter a baking dish, and pour in pudding. Bake for 30 to 40 minutes.

*8 servings*

*"Tues. Dec. 25th 1804. . . . Seth Baker has arrived with the cranberries. [Seth and his cranberries had been expected a day or two sooner; perhaps he was detained at Hyannis by a head wind.] As his arrival is noised through the town, housekeeping women are hastening to the wharf, carrying baskets and pails to be filled with cranberries for their Christmas dinners."* Quaint Nantucket, *William Root Bliss*

# ANNA COFFIN'S SECOND DAY
# WEDDING PUDDING

10 ounces crackers
6 cups milk
½ pound butter, softened
1 cup sugar

2 cups raisins, boiled
1 teaspoon salt
½ teaspoon grated nutmeg
10 eggs, well beaten

Preheat oven to 325° F.

Pound the crackers fine. Boil the milk and pour onto crackers.

Cream the butter, add the sugar, and beat. Add to the crackers and milk. Add raisins, salt and nutmeg. Cool.

Add well-beaten eggs. Pour into well-buttered 3½-quart baking dish. Bake for 1¼ hours.

Serve with Brandy Sauce (recipe follows).

*about 16 servings*

BRANDY SAUCE

1 cup sugar
2 cups water
2 tablespoons cornstarch

2 tablespoons cold water
2 tablespoons brandy

Put sugar in water and bring to a boil. Add cornstarch that has been mixed with cold water, and stir until the mixture is clear.

Remove from heat and add brandy.

*about 2½ cups sauce*

*In a handwritten notebook along with formulas for cold creams and Colognes was this recommendation for the cure of cholera, obviously a mistaken assumption:*

*"First drink pure cognac brandy one half pint. Then every fifteen minutes after take one tablespoonful of a mixture made of ½ oz. each of gum myrrh, cayenne pepper, and camphor—in a pint of pure cognac—for the first hour. It will cure either the gripes or colic instantly."*

# WHITPOT

In *Nantucket Cook Book* there is a recipe for this dish that goes as follows: "Some people like this for dessert as much as other dislike it. One quart of milk, one egg, one tablespoonful of meal (Indian), two table-spoonfuls of flour, not heaped, one half cup molasses. Boil half the milk, add a little salt; mix the other ingredients with the rest of the milk cold. Pour this into the boiling milk without stirring. Set in a moderate oven and let it bake till it is a little thicker than boiled custard."

In a cookbook we found another recipe for Whitpot which had "Indian" in parentheses after the name. "Take one quart sweet milk, one-half pint of Indian meal, two to three eggs, one-half teaspoon salt, and four tablespoons of sugar. Boil one pint of the milk, stir in the meal, stir in the meal while boiling, cook five minutes and add the remainder of the milk. Beat the sugar and eggs together, and when cold stir the whole thoroughly and bake one hour in a deep dish. To be eaten either hot or cold."

It appears that "Whitpot" was another name for Indian Pudding.

In the same book is a molasses or mock Whitpot which has the addition of ¼ pint of molasses, and cooking in the same manner. "A very cheap and good pudding easily made."

# *PIES*

Pies were a staple island dessert from the time Nantucket was settled, and remain so today. Flour and lard were always available for the crusts and there were wild berries and plums, domestic pumpkins and squash and apples. If none of these was available, there was always custard or lemon pie to make. Old recipes always used 1 lemon, both the juice and grated zest for flavoring.

Beach plums are still picked in late summer and fall, when ripe. Blueberries and blackberries in season, and strawberries in the spring.

Crusts were made of any variety of fat—from suet, lard, butter and now vegetable fats. Puff paste was made with a lot of butter, plain pastry with lard. Crusts were made of bread dough too.

What could be easier than to save a good piece of dough from the bread-making to cover a pie? One recipe made with boiling water was called "scalded crust." Then there were crusts made of baking powder biscuit dough and corn-bread crusts too.

The recipes that call for pastry for 1-crust pie use one quarter of the recipe that follows. Two 2-crust pies are the whole recipe, enough for 9-inch pie pans.

---

*"Puddings and pyes were a part of social life no liquor was ever served in early times by the plain people."* Nantucket, the Far-Away Island, *William Oliver Stevens*

---

## STANDARD PASTRY

4 cups flour
½ teaspoon baking powder
1 teaspoon salt

1 cup lard
¼ cup cold water

Sift flour, baking powder and salt.

Cut lard into flour, or mix lightly with fingers until mixture is as fine as cornmeal. Add water and shape into a ball.

Divide dough into 2 balls, one slightly larger than the other. Roll out ¼ to ⅛ inch thick on a floured board or cloth.

Place pie pan face down on dough. Cut dough 1 inch beyond lip all the way around. Fold over and remove from board to pan. Lay in pan and pat gently into place. Repeat to cut pastry circle for top crust, the width of the pan. Reserve.

Fill pan with filling and cover with top pastry. Crimp pastry edges together. Cut steam vents in top pastry.

Preheat oven to 375° F.

Bake pie for 15 minutes. Reduce heat to 325° and bake for 30 minutes more.

*pastry for two 2-crust pies*

# OLD-FASHIONED FLAKY PASTRY

The method of making this pastry is most unusual. It came from Portsmouth, New Hampshire, sent to the *Boston Herald* in 1906.

3½ cups flour
1 teaspoon salt
1 cup lard

2 eggs
6 tablespoons butter

Mix flour, salt and lard until mixture is as fine as cornmeal.

"In cold weather shave the lard as thin as possible so it will more easily rub into the flour. In very warm weather it should be handled carefully so as not to become greasy."

Beat the eggs in a bowl; add with enough water to wet the mixture of flour and lard. Transfer the dough to a breadboard and knead it well. Then roll it out about 1½ inches thick.

Work the butter on a plate with a knife until it is soft. Spread this evenly over the dough. Dust flour lightly over the butter, and sprinkle a very little water lightly over the flour. Then form the dough into a roll the shape of a rolling pin.

The pastry can be used immediately, or it can be refrigerated or frozen.

Cut from the roll, as one would slice jelly roll, enough for a single crust. If you wish layers to show rings, place flat on board and roll. If you wish layers to have a crosswise appearance place outer edge on board and roll out this way.

Bake to a golden brown. Crust will be soft and cut well even when hot. Delicious for meat or chicken pie. For meat pies cut about 2 inches larger around than size of dish.

*pastry for 3 single crusts*

---

# APPLE GRUNT

2 tablespoons butter
6 medium-size apples, pared
    and quartered
¼ cup molasses
¼ cup sugar

½ teaspoon ground
    cinnamon
¼ cup water
1 recipe Skillet Biscuits (p.
    138) or Dumplings (p. 139)

Melt butter in a skillet. Add apples and molasses, and sprinkle with sugar and cinnamon. Add water and cook for a few minutes.

Mix biscuit dough or dumpling batter and drop on apples by tablespoons. Cover, and cook over medium-low heat, without lifting cover, for 15 minutes.

*6 to 8 servings* *quick*

## APPLE POTPIE

"Make your bread as usual. Let it rise." Bread was "put down" every evening. This was a simple pie to make the next day for dinner.

bread dough
1 teaspoon lard
6 to 8 apples, peeled and
    quartered

1 cup molasses
1 cup water

Preheat oven to 350° F.

Take enough of the risen bread dough to make a crust for a deep baking dish. Mix it with the teaspoon of lard. Roll out to size of pot.

Put the quartered apples in the baking dish. Pour molasses over apples and add water. Cover with bread dough.

Bake for 35 to 40 minutes, until the crust is brown.

*6 to 8 servings*

## BANBURY TARTS

½ recipe Standard Pastry
  (p. 172)
1 lemon
1 egg
1 cup sugar

1 cup raisins, chopped
1 tablespoon cornstarch
  stirred into 2 tablespoons
  water
2 tablespoons butter

Preheat oven to 400° F.

Roll out pastry ¼ inch or less thick. Cut into 6 squares, 3 by 3 inches.

Grate lemon rind and squeeze lemon juice. Mix egg, sugar, raisins, cornstarch and butter. Add lemon juice and grated rind.

Put a square of pastry on a large saucer. Put on this one sixth of the filling. Fold over the dough to make a triangle, and crimp well all around. Lay on cookie sheet. Repeat with all the squares.

Bake at 400° F. for 10 minutes, then reduce heat to 350°; bake for 15 to 20 minutes more.

*6 servings*

## BLUEBERRY PIE

2 cups blueberries
1 cup sugar
1 egg

pastry for 2-crust, 9-inch pie
  (p. 172)

Preheat oven to 400° F.

Mix blueberries, sugar and egg.

Line pie pan with pastry. Pour in blueberry mixture. Cover with top pastry, and crimp edges together. Make slits in top pastry.

Bake at 400° F. for 15 minutes, then reduce heat to 350° and bake for another 20 to 30 minutes, or until juice boils up through vents and pie is brown.

*6 servings*

# BEACH PLUM PIE

Beach plums are a tart berrylike fruit and are made into jelly, jam, relish, conserve, pie. They require more sugar than other fruits, at least ¾ cup per cup of plums.

2 cups ripe beach plums, washed
1½ cups sugar
sour cream

grated rind of 1 orange or 1 lemon
pastry for 2-crust, 9-inch pie (p. 172)

Preheat oven to 375° F.

Remove pits from beach plums. Add sugar and orange rind to plums.

Line 9-inch pie pan with half of pastry. Pour sugared plums into pastry-lined pan. Cover with top pastry, crimp edges, and cut vents in top.

Bake for 10 minutes. Reduce heat to 325° and bake for 20 to 30 minutes longer, until juice bubbles out of vents. Serve with a spoonful of sour cream.

*6 servings*

---

# BRANT'S PIE

2 cups cranberries
1 cup raisins, cut into halves and boiled for 30 minutes

1 cup sugar
1 teaspoon vanilla extract
pastry for 2-crust 9-inch pie (p. 172)

Preheat oven to 375° F.

Mix cranberries, raisins, sugar and vanilla. Cook for 10 minutes. Cool.

Pour the mixture into pastry-lined pie pan. Cover with top pastry and crimp around the edges; (or cover with lattice strips). Make 3 vents in top pastry.

Bake for 10 minutes, then reduce heat to 325° and bake for another 30 minutes, or until juice boils through the vents and the pie is brown.

*6 servings*                                                          *quick*

## LEMON CREAM PIE

1 egg, beaten
2 tablespoons cornstarch or
    flour
2 tablespoons sugar

⅛ teaspoon salt
2 cups milk
1 teaspoon lemon extract
pastry for 2-crust pie (p. 172)

Mix egg, cornstarch, sugar and salt. Add milk gradually.

Cook in top part of a double boiler over hot water until thick. Add lemon extract. Cool.

Roll out pastry to 2 rounds. Bake each round separately.

Lay 1 crust on a serving plate. Cover with the cooled custard, and top with second crust.

*6 servings*     *quick*

---

## LEMON TARTS

1 large lemon, grated rind
    and juice
2 eggs
1 tablespoon butter

1 cup sugar
1 recipe Standard Pastry
    (p. 172)

Grate lemon rind and squeeze lemon juice. Add eggs, butter and sugar and beat well.

Put mixture into top part of a double boiler over boiling water and cook, stirring constantly, until mixture is thick, about 20 minutes.

To make tart shells: Roll out the pastry to a thin sheet. Cut out rounds to fit over 8 muffin tin bottoms. Cut remaining pastry into 8 small rounds and arrange flat on a baking sheet. Bake both muffin-shaped rounds and flat rounds for 10 to 12 minutes.

Fill baked shells with lemon mixture, and cover with the small pastry rounds.

*8 tarts*

## MINCE PIE WITHOUT MEAT

Quaker cooking was simple. Usually meat, apples and cider were added to this recipe. For a more elaborate mincemeat see page 186.

5 common crackers, or
    3 Boston crackers
½ cup milk
1 cup brown sugar
½ cup molasses
½ cup vinegar
¼ pound butter, softened

½ cup water
2 cups raisins, boiled
¾ teaspoon each of ground
    cloves and cinnamon
pastry for 2-crust 9-inch pie
    (p. 172)

Soak crackers in milk. Add sugar and molasses.

Preheat oven to 375° F.

Mix vinegar, butter, water and raisins; bring to a boil, and set aside. Add spices to cracker mixture. Combine two mixtures.

Pour into pastry-lined pie pan; cover with the top round of pastry. Crimp edges. Cut 3 vents in the top.

Bake for 10 minutes; reduce heat to 325° F. and bake for 35 to 45 minutes longer.

Serve hot with Hard Sauce (p. 162), flavored with bourbon.

*8 servings*

## GREEN TOMATO PIE

1 large green tomato,
    chopped
1 large apple, cored and
    chopped
½ cup raisins
1 lunch cracker, pounded
    fine
2 tablespoons vinegar

¼ teaspoon each of ground
    cloves, cinnamon and
    allspice
¾ cup firmly packed brown
    sugar
pastry for 2-crust, 8-inch pie
    (p. 172)

Preheat oven to 400° F.

Mix tomato, apple, raisins, cracker crumbs, vinegar, spices and brown sugar.

Line pie pan with half of pastry; put in filling. Cover with remaining pastry. Crimp well and cut vents in top.

Bake for 10 minutes. Reduce heat to 350° and bake for 20 to 30 minutes more, or until filling boils up through vents.

*4 servings*                                                              *quick*

## ORANGE CHIFFON PIE

2 tablespoons butter, softened
1 cup sugar
2 eggs, separated, yolks and
    whites beaten separately
3½ tablespoons flour

2 oranges, grated rinds and
    juice
1 cup milk
pastry for 1-crust 8-inch pie
    (p. 172)

Preheat oven to 375° F.

Cream butter; add the sugar, beaten egg yolks and flour.

Grate rinds of oranges and add. Add juice of oranges, stir, and add the milk. Fold in beaten egg whites.

Line pie pan with pastry; crimp edges. Pour the filling into pie pan.

Bake for 10 minutes. Reduce heat to 300° F. and bake until pie is light brown and filling is thickened, 30 to 40 minutes longer.

*6 servings*

## PUMPKIN PIE

1 small fresh pumpkin, or
    2 cups canned pumpkin
1 cup hot milk
2 eggs, beaten
½ cup sugar

½ teaspoon each of ground
    ginger and cinnamon
½ teaspoon grated nutmeg
pastry for 1-crust 9-inch pie
    (p. 172)

Preheat oven to 350° F.

Cut up pumpkin and bake until soft. Scrape pumpkin from skin and measure 2 cups for pie. (Freeze remainder.)

Combine all ingredients but nutmeg and pastry, and pour into pastry-lined pie pan. Sprinkle nutmeg over top.

Bake for 35 to 40 minutes, until a knife comes out clean when inserted into the custard. Serve warm or cold.

*6 servings*

## RHUBARB CUSTARD PIE

pastry for 1-crust 9-inch pie
(p. 172)
2 cups diced rhubarb
1 cup sugar

½ teaspoon grated nutmeg
2 eggs, separated
1 cup milk

Preheat oven to 375° F.

Line pie pan with pastry and crimp edges. Fill with diced rhubarb. Sprinkle with half the sugar and the nutmeg. Put in oven.

Mix egg yolks, milk and remaining sugar. Cook in top part of a double boiler over hot water until custard is thick. Set aside.

Beat egg whites until thick. Fold into custard. Remove pie from oven. Spoon custard over pie.

Reduce heat to 300° F. and bake for 20 to 30 minutes, or until custard is set.

*6 servings*

## STRAWBERRY PIE

4 cups strawberries
1 baked 9-inch pie shell
1 cup confectioners' sugar

½ teaspoon vanilla extract
1 egg white, beaten stiff

Preheat oven to 325° F.

Wash and pick over strawberries. Drain.

Set berries in circles in the baked pie shell. Sprinkle with ½ cup confectioners' sugar.

Add remaining confectioners' sugar and vanilla to stiff egg white. Drop this meringue by tablespoons onto strawberries.

Bake for 15 to 20 minutes, until meringue is light golden in color.

*6 servings*

## VINEGAR PIE

2 tablespoons flour
2 tablespoons sugar
1 egg
½ cup cider vinegar

1 cup molasses
2 tablespoons lemon extract
pastry for 1-crust 9-inch pie
(p. 172)

Preheat oven to 400° F.

Mix flour and sugar, add egg, then vinegar, molasses and lemon extract.

Pour into pastry-lined pie pan. Bake at 400° F. for 10 minutes. Reduce heat to 350°, and continue baking for 25 to 30 minutes.

*6 servings*                                                                 *quick*

## BLACKBERRY ROLL

1 recipe dough for Skillet
   Biscuits (p. 138)
6 cups ripe blackberries,
   washed

1 cup granulated sugar
¼ pound butter, softened
½ teaspoon vanilla extract
1½ tablespoons brandy

Preheat oven to 400° F.

Divide dough into 2 parts and roll each part to a sheet ⅛ inch thick. Lay one in a deep baking dish. Put in berries, level, and cover with the other sheet of dough. Crimp edges. Bake for 30 minutes.

Make hard sauce: beat sugar into softened butter until thick and creamy. Add vanilla and brandy. Beat again. Serve with blackberry roll.

*6 to 8 servings*

*By the Quaker calendar: Sunday is the 1st day*
*Monday the 2nd day*
*Tuesday the 3rd day*
*Wednesday the 4th day*
*Thursday the 5th day*
*Friday the 6th day*
*Saturday the 7th day*

*Quaker verse to replace the familiar "30 days hath September, April, June, and November," etc.:*
*The ninth, the eleventh, the fourth, the sixth*
*Have thirty-days to each affixed*
*All the rest have thirty-one,*
*Except the second alone*
*Which hath twenty-eight,*
*Excepting leap year (once in four)*
*When it hath one day more.*

# PICKLES,
# PRESERVES
# & CANDIES

## TOMATO KETCHUP

1 peck (8 quarts) ripe
    tomatoes
3 tablespoons salt
1 tablespoon each of black
    pepper and ground
    cloves, cinnamon and
    allspice

½ tablespoon cayenne pepper
2 cups vinegar
1 cup sugar
1 teaspoon celery seeds

Chop tomatoes. Add remaining ingredients and bring to a boil. Reduce heat and simmer for 2 hours.

Pour into hot sterilized jars. Cover, but do not seal until cool.

*about 10 quarts*

---

## GRAPE KETCHUP

5 pounds grapes
2½ pounds sugar
1 tablespoon each of ground
    cinnamon, cloves and
    allspice

½ tablespoon salt
1 tablespoon pepper

Pick over grapes, remove stems, and wash. Put into a saucepan with only the water that clings to them. Cook until skins burst.

Add remaining ingredients and boil down to the consistency desired. Put into sterilized jars and store in a cool place. Serve with fish and shellfish.

*6 or 7 pints*

## PLAIN CHILI SAUCE

6 ripe tomatoes, skinned
2 small green peppers
2 onions

1½ cups cider vinegar
1 tablespoon sugar
1 tablespoon salt

Chop tomatoes, peppers and onions. Add vinegar, sugar and salt.

Simmer all together until all the water has evaporated, about 2 hours. Bottle in sterilized jars.

*about 2 pints*

## SPICY CHILI SAUCE

32 ripe tomatoes, chopped
7 peppers, seeded and
   chopped
7 onions, peeled and
   chopped
2 cups vinegar
½ cup sugar

7 teaspoons salt
1½ tablespoons each of
   ground cinnamon, ginger
   and allspice
1½ tablespoons grated
   nutmeg

Chop tomatoes, peppers and onions, discarding stems, seeds, etc.

Bring all to a boil together, reduce heat, and cook for 2 hours.

*about 10 quarts*

## PICKLED QUINCES

5 pounds quinces
2 pounds sugar
2 cups white vinegar

2 tablespoons each of whole
   cloves and pieces of
   cinnamon stick

Peel and core the quinces, leaving whole if possible; if very large, quarter them.

Cover with enough water to cook them, and simmer gently until tender. Remove each quince from water and drain; reserve cooking liquid.

Add sugar to cooking liquid with vinegar, cloves and cinnamon. Bring to a boil and cook for 5 minutes.

Put quinces into sterilized jars and fill jars with syrup. Put on covers. Let stand until cool. Seal and keep in a cool place.

*5 or 6 pints*

---

## MINCEMEAT

Lucretia Mott, a pioneer for women's rights, was often criticized for neglecting her family. Here is a quote from her diary in an old Nantucket book. "Up at dawn to pick peas. Mended stockings before breakfast, and made mince for 40 pies, doing every part myself even to meat chopping. Picked over apples stewed a quantity, and made apple pudding. Before noon went to printing office where a number of women were employed. Hadn't my shawl and bonnet off, before five arrived for dinner. Afterward sat for an artist who desires my portrait. After tea turned shirts and hemmed towels." *Island Patchwork,* Eleanor Early

This is not Miss Mott's mincemeat but it might have been.

| | |
|---|---|
| 3½ pounds lean beef, cooked | 2 tablespoons salt |
| 2 pounds beef suet | 2 cups sweet cider |
| 3 quarts chopped apples | ⅓ teaspoon each of ground |
| 2 pounds raisins |     cloves, allspice and |
| 1 pound dried currants |     cinnamon |
| juice of 3 oranges | 1 teaspoon each of grated |
| juice of 3 lemons |     mace and nutmeg |
| 2 cups sugar | 1 cup molasses |

Mix all together and simmer for 2 hours.

Put in 5 sterilized quart jars and process for 30 minutes.

## BLUEBERRY CONSERVE

1 whole lemon, chopped,
  seeds removed
1 whole orange, chopped,
  seeds removed
½ pound seedless raisins

4 pounds sugar
2 quarts blueberries, washed
2 cups water
1 cup chopped walnuts

Put the lemon, orange and raisins through a meat grinder, using the coarse blade.

Add the sugar, blueberries and water. Cover and cook over very low heat, stirring often to prevent burning, until mixture is thick, about 45 minutes.

Stir in the walnuts and pack into jars. Cover and store in a cool place.

*about 4 quarts*

---

## BEACH PLUM JELLY

A most delicious jelly can be made with these wild plums found in Nantucket and Cape Cod. They ripen around the end of August.

4 cups mixed ripe and unripe
  beach plums

3½ cups sugar,
  approximately

Cook plums in water to cover until pulp is soft and stones separate from fruit. The unripe fruit adds pectin and helps the mixture to jell.

Mash plums in pot and pour fruit into a jelly bag or a piece of unbleached muslin over a bowl; tie opposite ends and suspend over the bowl. Squeeze gently, then let drip until it stops. Don't let pulp come through cheesecloth or jelly will be cloudy.

Measure juice and allow ¾ cup sugar to each cup of juice. Boil juice and sugar to 220° F. on a candy thermometer, or until a few drops flow together and hang from the spoon in a sheet. Skim.

Pour into hot sterilized glasses. Cool. Seal glasses with paraffin. Let cool and seal again.

*4 or 5 glasses, 8-ounce size*

# ROSE HIP JELLY

Pick wild rose hips when their color turns at the end of August.

| | |
|---|---|
| 2 cups rose hips | 5 cups sugar, approximately |
| 4 cups water | 1 box (1¾ ounces) pectin or |
| 5 underripe or sour apples |    ½ bottle (6-ounce size) |
| 2½ cups water | |

Remove stem ends and wash rose hips. Cover with 4 cups water and bring to a boil. Simmer until rose hips are soft.

Mash and pour into a jelly bag. Make a jelly bag with cheesecloth doubled or a square of cotton-wool flannel, and tie opposite corners together. Let drip over a bowl overnight.

Wash apples; do not peel or core. Cover with 2½ cups water, and follow directions for rose hips. Let drip overnight.

Measure juices. To each cup of rose hip juice, add ½ cup of apple juice. To each cup of the combined juices measure ⅔ to 1 cup sugar. Put all in a large kettle. Add pectin.

Bring to a rapid rolling boil for 6 or 7 minutes, 220° F. on a candy thermometer, or until juice drops in sheets and 2 drops hang from spoon. Remove from heat.

Skim jelly and pour into sterilized hot glasses. Cool slightly and cover with melted paraffin.

*about 10 glasses, 6-ounce size*

---

# BEACH PLUM JAM

| | |
|---|---|
| 4 cups beach plums | grated rind of 1 lemon |
| 3 cups sugar | |

Wash and pit plums. Simmer in water to cover until plums are soft.

Add sugar and lemon rind, and simmer over low heat until thick.

Skim. Pour into sterilized jars and seal with melted paraffin.

Cool, and seal again. Store in a cool place.

*about 5 glasses, 8-ounce size*

# WILD GRAPE JELLY

Wild grapes grow in profusion on Nantucket. They make an excellent jelly if one has the patience to gather them. The flavor of wild grapes is much more intense than that of the cultivated grape, but the recipe for making the jelly is the same.

| | |
|---|---|
| 4 quarts grapes, about 2 pounds | 3 cups sugar, approximately |
| 3 cups water | spice bag (optional) |

Pick over grapes, remove the stems, and wash. Put into a large kettle and crush thoroughly. Add 3 cups water, bring to a boil, and simmer for 15 to 20 minutes.

Put into a jelly bag and squeeze and hang until all juice is extracted, 3 to 4 cups.

Measure juice and add ¾ cup sugar to each cup juice. Cook until sugar is dissolved. Add spice bag, if used.

Boil rapidly for 20 minutes, or until 2 thick drops come off of spoon, 220° F. on a candy thermometer.

Pour into hot sterilized glasses, cool slightly, and seal with melted paraffin. Cool and seal again.

*3 to 5 glasses, 8-ounce size*

---

# CRANBERRY CLARET JELLY

| | |
|---|---|
| 1 cup fresh cranberries | 1 cup claret wine |
| ½ cup water | ½ bottle fruit pectin (6-ounce size) |
| 3½ cups sugar | |

Put cranberries and ½ cup water into a pot, bring to a boil, and cook for 10 minutes. Strain off 1 cup of the juice and put into the top part of a double boiler, reserving the berries for another use.

Add sugar and wine, place over rapidly boiling water in the lower pot, and cook, stirring, for 2 minutes, or until sugar is dissolved.

Remove from heat, skim, and stir in the pectin. Pour into sterilized jars, seal with melted paraffin, cool, and seal again.

*about 4 jars, 8-ounce size*

## CRANBERRY CONSERVE

4 cups cranberries
⅔ cup cold water
⅔ cup boiling water
½ cup seeded raisins

1 orange, thinly sliced and
  chopped
3 cups granulated sugar
1 cup chopped walnuts

Pick over and wash the cranberries. Add ⅔ cup cold water and bring to a boil. Cook for 10 minutes, or until skins burst. Put through a food mill.

Add ⅔ cup boiling water, the raisins, orange and sugar to puréed cranberries. Return to a boil, and simmer for 20 minutes. Stir in the chopped nuts.

Pour into hot sterilized glasses. Seal with melted paraffin, cool, and seal again.

*6 to 8 glasses, 8-ounce size*

---

## BUTTERSCOTCH TAFFY

2 cups white sugar
2 tablespoons vinegar

1 teaspoon vanilla extract
1 tablespoon butter

Put all the ingredients into a saucepan. Boil until a drop of the mixture hardens in water (290° F. on a candy thermometer). Cool until it will not burn hands.

Butter hands, pick up a chunk of candy, and pull as one would a hank of yarn. Cut or break into bite-size pieces.

*1 pound*                                                                 *quick*

---

*From a shutter on a local grocery store, the* Inquirer *of October 5th, 1833.* Quaint Nantucket, *William Root Bliss*

> *New Cider Sweat and good*
> *Pleas to trye it if you would*
> *Apples Paires and Peaches too*
> *As good fruite as ever grew*
> *Oysters fine as ever you saw*
> *You can have them cook'd or take them raw.*

## HICKORY NUT CANDY

1½ pounds sugar                    1½ cups shelled hickory nuts
½ cup milk

Boil sugar and milk for 10 minutes. Remove from heat and stir until white.

Add hickory nuts. Pour into a tin lined with buttered paper. Cool, and cut into 2-inch squares.

*about 2 pounds candy*                                    *quick*

---

## MAPLE SUGAR CANDY

1½ cups maple sugar            2 tablespoons butter
1½ cups white sugar            1 cup chopped walnuts
1 cup milk

Put the sugars, milk and butter into a saucepan. Boil until the syrup spins a thread, 234° F. on a candy thermometer. Remove from heat and beat until creamy.

Add nuts, and pour into a buttered tin. Cool and cut into 2-inch squares.

*about 2 pounds candy*                                    *quick*

## MINNIE COFFIN'S SOUR-CREAM CANDY

1 cup sour cream
2 cups light brown sugar

1 cup nuts—pecans, walnuts,
  or other

Cook sour cream and sugar together until the mixture forms a soft ball when dropped into a cup of cold water. Add nuts.

Pour into a pie tin to cool. Score with a knife while hot.

*1 pound* *quick*

## NUT TAFFY

1 cup molasses
1 cup sugar
1 ounce (1 square) chocolate

2 tablespoons milk
3 tablespoons butter
¾ cup nut meats, broken

Put the molasses, sugar, chocolate, milk and butter into a saucepan. Cook until a small portion becomes brittle when dropped into cold water, 256° F. on a candy thermometer.

Remove from heat and stir in nut meats. Pour into a buttered pan. Cool, and cut into 2-inch squares.

*about 1 pound taffy* *quick*

## PEPPERMINTS

1 pound sugar
6 tablespoons water

10 drops oil of peppermint

Boil sugar and water together for 4 minutes. Add peppermint. Beat until creamy.

Drop by teaspoons onto a marble slab, wax paper or aluminum foil.

*about 30 mints* *quick*

# BEVERAGES

## BLOODY MARY

½ ounce (1 tablespoon) fresh
   lemon juice
dash of Worcestershire sauce
dash of Tabasco

4 ounces (½ cup) tomato
   juice
salt and pepper
1½ ounces vodka

Put all the ingredients into a cocktail shaker and shake well. Strain into a 6-ounce glass.

*1 serving*

---

## BULLSHOT

3 ounces condensed beef
   bouillon, or 1 packet
   powdered beef extract
   and 6 tablespoons water
⅛ teaspoon Worcestershire
   sauce

⅛ teaspoon Tabasco
juice of ½ lemon
1½ ounces vodka or gin
ice cubes

Put bouillon in highball glass, or dissolve extract in water in bottom of glass.

Add Worcestershire, Tabasco, lemon juice and vodka. Fill glass with ice cubes, stir, and serve.

*1 serving*

## MULLED CIDER

1 quart apple cider
2 whole cloves
2 whole allspice berries

1 cinnamon stick
½ cup brown sugar

Mix together all the ingredients and simmer for 10 minutes. Serve hot in mugs.

*6 servings*

## COFFEE CARIOCA

2 tablespoons sugar
rind of 1 orange, sliced (zest)
¼ cup finely ground coffee
   beans

2 cups boiling water
½ cup dark rum
¼ cup sweetened whipped
   cream

Place the sugar, orange rind and ground coffee in a heatproof bowl. Stir in boiling water and let stand for 30 minutes.

Strain into a coffeepot and heat to just under boiling. Stir in rum, and pour into demitasse cups.

Serve topped with whipped cream and a little grated orange rind.

*4 servings*

## IRISH COFFEE

The Irish make this with 2 teaspoons each of brown and white sugar and unwhipped real fresh cream, thicker than our heaviest cream.

2 teaspoons sugar
1 ounce Irish whiskey
strong black coffee

2 tablespoons whipped cream
   or heavy cream, or more

Put the sugar and whiskey into a wineglass. Fill almost to the top with strong black coffee, stir, and top with cream.

After six or seven of these, who minds the cold New England nights?

*1 serving*

## CLARET CUP

1 quart claret                ½ lemon, sliced
¼ cup sugar                  1 quart cold soda water
½ orange, sliced

Mix wine, sugar and fruits together in a large pitcher. Add ice, stir well, and add the soda water.

*20 servings*

## CRANBERRY PUNCH

In early Nantucket times this spicy drink was served hot in mugs.

4 pounds cranberries          4 cups orange juice
4 cups sugar                  1 cup lemon juice
2 quarts water                1 quart light rum
12 cinnamon sticks            orange and lemon slices
24 whole cloves

Put the cranberries, sugar, water, cinnamon and cloves into a kettle, cover, and cook until cranberries are soft.

Strain, cool the liquid, and pour into a punch bowl containing a cake of ice.

Add the fruit juices and the rum. Garnish with orange and lemon slices and ladle over the ice until well chilled. If desired, the punch may be diluted by adding soda water or ginger ale.

*5 quarts*

## CRANBERRY COCKTAIL

6 ounces (¾ cup) cranberry
   juice

6 ounces vodka
dash of Cointreau

Put all the ingredients into a shaker with cracked ice and shake well.

Serve in chilled cocktail glasses with a cranberry in each.

*4 servings*

## DANDELION WINE

1 gallon dandelion blossoms,
   stems removed
1 gallon water
4 pounds sugar

5 oranges, cut up
3 lemons, cut up
1 cake or envelope yeast,
   dissolved in ½ cup water

Put the dandelion blossoms into a large kettle, pour in the gallon of water, and cover with a cloth. Allow to stand at room temperature for 2 days.

Bring to a boil and cook, covered, for 20 minutes. Strain into a large crock.

Add the sugar, oranges and lemons. Cover with a cloth and allow to cool to room temperature.

Stir in the yeast, cover again, and allow to stand for 1 week.

Strain again. Return liquid to the crock, and allow to stand until fermentation process stops (no bubbles).

Syphon into bottles and cap or cork.

*about 5 quarts wine*

## ELDERBERRY WINE

Elderberry wine has a delightfully rich flavor that can be spoiled by fermenting too quickly. For this reason it is preferable not to add yeast as in making dandelion wine. (If you can't wait, ½ teaspoon of brewer's yeast will speed fermentation.)

1 gallon elderberries, cleaned      12 cups sugar
1 gallon water      2 cups brandy (optional)

Put the elderberries and water into a large kettle, bring to a boil, and simmer for 10 minutes. Mash.

Strain through a cloth into a large crock and stir in the sugar until dissolved. (Less sugar can be used for tart wine.)

Cover with a cloth and allow to stand at room temperature, skimming from time to time, until clear, about 15 days.

When fermentation has stopped—when bubbles cease to rise to the top, this is the time to add the brandy if you use it. With or without brandy, syphon into bottles and cap or cork. The wine is better if drunk after 6 months.

*about 5 quarts wine*

---

## CHRISTMAS EGGNOG

Eggnog is best when mellowed for several days before serving.

6 eggs      2 cups bourbon whiskey
½ cup sugar      ½ cup rum
¼ teaspoon salt      grated nutmeg
2 cups heavy cream, whipped

In a large bowl beat the eggs until foamy. Add the sugar and salt, continuing to beat until thickened.

Stir in the whipped cream, then the bourbon and rum. Chill until ready for use.

Ladle from bowl into glass cups and serve sprinkled with nutmeg.

*12 servings*

---

## GROG

The dictionary says that the name of this drink came from "Old Grog. (alluding to his *grogram* cloak), the nickname of Edward Vernon (d. 1757) British admiral, who in 1740 ordered the alcholic mixture to be served instead of pure spirits, to the sailors."

Later it was served with hot tea. The ration was usually one gill (¼ pint) per man.

1 teaspoon sugar        1 lemon slice
boiling tea or water
¼ pint (½ cup) rum or
     whisky

Put sugar in bottom of mug or 8-ounce glass. Stir with a spoon; leave spoon in glass to prevent breakage. Fill two-thirds full with tea. Fill remaining space with rum, add lemon, and stir.

*1 serving*

## HARPOON

1½ ounces (1 jigger) vodka      1 slice of orange
2 ounces (¼ cup) sweetened
     cranberry juice

Fill an old-fashioned glass with ice cubes. Add vodka, then cranberry juice. Garnish with slice of orange and serve.

*1 serving*

*"Cranberry juice cocktail was used on here long before it was in general use."*

## MOONSHOT

1½ ounces vodka      dash of Tabasco
3 ounces clam juice

Fill an old-fashioned glass with ice cubes. Add vodka, clam juice and Tabasco. Stir and serve.

*1 serving*

## HOT RUM PUNCH

Nantucketers have long used this old New England drink to serve at parties during the cold winter evenings.

2 quarts cider
6 ounces heavy dark rum
3 cinnamon sticks

¼ teaspoon grated mace
½ teaspoon ground allspice

Mix all the ingredients, heat, and serve in mugs.

*about 20 servings*

## HOT BUTTERED RUM

In colonial taverns this was heated by plunging a hot poker into the mug.

1 teaspoon brown sugar
2 ounces rum
4 ounces (½ cup) hard cider

1 tablespoon butter
$^1/_{16}$ teaspoon grated nutmeg

Put sugar into a mug. Add rum; stir. Heat cider. Add butter. When very hot pour into mug. Serve dusted with nutmeg.

*1 serving*

## MINT TEA

Fresh mint grows wild in New England along brooks and beside lakes and is cultivated in gardens. It is dried for winter use in sauce and mint tea. It is brisk and refreshing.

4 tablespoons mint leaves
4 cups boiling water

1½ ounces (1 jigger) rum per
   cup (optional)

Put mint in teapot. Pour in boiling water and steep for 3 to 5 minutes, according to taste. Serve with sugar or rock candy on the side. Add rum if desired.

*4 servings*

## WINE CASSIS

4 ounces dry white wine,
   chilled

½ ounce crème de cassis

Pour into chilled wineglass and serve.

*1 serving*

## *ACKNOWLEDGMENTS*

Our thanks to these residents of Nantucket for their help and contributions.

Theresa Anderson
Nathaniel Benchley
Peggy Coote
Amanda and Harlan Davis
Louise Gibson
Hank Kellenbeck
Jane Lamb
Beverley and Harold Lindley
Claudette Pearl

Rosalie and Albert Pitkin
Maxie Ryder
Charlie Sayle
Annette Stackpole
Florence Stackpole
Jon Stroup
Esther Swain
Alicia and Pete Watrous

also thanks to mothers, grandmothers and friends who preserved many handwritten recipes.

# REFERENCES

Bliss, William Root, *Quaint Nantucket,* Houghton Mifflin Company, Boston, 1896.

Early, Eleanor, *Island Patchwork,* Houghton Mifflin Company, Boston, 1941.

Franklin, Benjamin, *The Autobiography of Benjamin Franklin.*

Gibbons, Euell, *Stalking the Blue-Eyed Scallop,* David McKay Company, New York, 1964.

Macy, William F., and Hussey, Roland B., eds., *The Nantucket Scrap Basket,* The Inquirer and Mirror Press, Nantucket, 1916.

Melville, Herman, *Moby-Dick or The Whale.*

Starbuck, Mary Eliza, *My House and I; A Chronicle of Nantucket,* Houghton Mifflin Company, Boston, 1929.

Stevens, William Oliver, *Nantucket, the Far-Away Island,* Dodd, Mead & Company, New York, 1936.

*Nantucket Cook Book,* The Inquirer and Mirror Press, Nantucket, from *Nantucket Receipts,* compiled by Mrs. Susan C. Hosmer for the benefit of the Nantucket Atheneum, 1874; later recipes were added by Miss Caroline L. Tallant, and again by Mrs. Maria L. Owen, 1915. A later edition was edited by Harry D. Turner, 1927. (courtesy of Mrs. Charles Stackpole)

*Recipes* (recipes contributed by Boston housewives), an advertising booklet, A. H. Hartley & Co., Boston.

Women's Forum for Cooking Recipes and Household Suggestions, *Boston Sunday Post,* February 18, 1906.

# INDEX